Author of:

1.) "Correcting Distortions of The Bible"
2.) "The Purpose of The Fall"
3.) "The Law of One- Condensed: Book 1"
4.) "The Law of One- Condensed: Book 2"
5.) "The Law of One- Condensed: Book 3"
6.) "The Law of One- Condensed: Book 4"
7.) "The Law of One- Condensed: Book 5"

Shop for Charity:

http://author-kathryn-jordyn.printify.me/

Law of One: Condensed

BOOK #5

(Easier to Read & Understand)

By: Kathryn Jordyn

Copyright © 2024 by Kathryn Jordyn

Published by Kathryn Jordyn

Published on planet Earth in the Milky Way Galaxy.

All rights reserved. No part of this publication may be reproduced, stored in a retrieval system or transmitted in any form by any means, electronic, mechanical, photocopy, recording, or otherwise, except as provided by USA copyright law.

Cover design and Illustration by Kathryn Jordyn

Printed in the United States of America

ISBN- 978-1-7350438-8-3

Episode 103:

Sometimes negative entities can speak to someone giving upcoming cataclysmic earth changes (which is something violently destructive such as a volcano, flood or earthquake and), false information and dates (such as negative entities giving so-called prophets false information and false dates). Then, when made public by the group receiving such information, makes the group lose credibility since the dates are never correct. Thus, the negative entity takes the spiritual strength of the light that the group had been able to share in service-to-others work.

Typically, one can challenge the entity giving information through the instrument by demanding to know if they came in the name of Jesus the Christ, Christ Consciousness, the positive polarity, service to others or in the name of one of the archangels or in whatever represents the center of one's life. This forms a wall of light through which a negative entity has trouble passing through like a brick wall. A group can also walk the Circle of One to replace the challenging procedure used in telepathic channeling, since one can immediately go into a trance state, out of body, and unaware of any activity.

The group used "tuned trance telepathy" to communicate with Ra. While the contact was underway, neither Carla nor those of Ra inhabited Carla's body. Carla's spirit was in the care of those of Ra while Ra used Carla's body from a distance to form the words that responded to Don's questions (the questioner).

Don Elkins was born in 1930 and died in 1984. He held a Master of Science in mechanical engineering and was a Wanderer here on Earth, which is a being that comes from higher densities back into our 3rd density world to be of service. He was a professor of physics, Boeing Pilot, US Army master sergeant during the Korean War and started his experiments in channeling in 1962, using protocols he used from a contactee group in Michigan.

(I notice that channeling in 2024 does not have those psychic attacks when they are in the trance state, unaware of what's going on. Perhaps this is safer since the higher 6th density more evolved beings are giving the information and in control of the body, whereas in tuned trance Carla was aware and therefore susceptible to demon attacks, even though they didn't physically hurt her.)

The groups meditation before each session was their group process of tuning. Ra mentioned many times that they had only the grossest control over her body and had difficulty, for example, in repositioning her hands when experiencing pain flares due to her arthritic condition. Carla could not feel the pain flares, but repositioning them when pain occurred helped get rid of the static on the line (her pain was due to her arthritis and not from negative entity attacks.)

Don and Carla worked together for 12 years, channeling, researching and writing two books in metaphysics before Jim joined them in 1980 and three weeks later the Ra contact occurred. It happened when Carla was conducting a teaching session, when one of the Sunday meditation group members was learning how to channel.

The reception of Ra's beam is somewhat more advanced than some of the broader vibration channels opened by others for more introductory and intermediate work.

Before a channeling Session: Ra recommended that each entity have the appropriate attitude in seeking this information and be in harmony with each other before attending any session. One example was Don explaining to Jim the meaning of the Bible, candle, incense, and chalice of water held for them as triggering mechanisms or signals to their subconscious minds that a session was about to take place, and that from all levels of their being they should begin the process of purifying their desires to serve others above all else and to surround ourself with joy-filled light of praise and thanksgiving. The harmony that this process produced among the group was as a musical cord where Ra could blend their vibrations, and upon the harmonious bend of vibrations, information of a metaphysical nature could be transmitted by being drawn to those who sought it.

Episode 104: Conspiracy theories that have to do with unseen groups and individuals who are said to be real powers behind governments and their activities in the world today are true. Such theories usually hold that the news reports that we hear and read concerning politics, economics, the military and so forth are but the tip of a very large iceberg that has mainly to do with various schemes for world domination and that functions through secret activities of a small elite group of human beings and their alien allies, the negative density aliens, since the negative path is control, manipulation, wars, domination over others ect. Focusing on conspiracy theories and those elites involved tends to reinforce the illusion of separation and ignores the love that binds all things as One being.

Ra communicating through a "narrow band wavelength" means that only information of the purest and most precise nature concerning the process of the evolution of mind, body and spirit could be successfully transmitted on a sustainable basis through our instrument. It also means that it's more advanced information.

Ra: "There is a certain amount of landing taking place. Some of these landings are of your own people; some are of the group known to you as Orion."

*Elites on Earth has the technology achievement of being able to create and fly unidentified flying objects. Unfortunately for the social memory complex vibratory rate of your peoples, these devices are not intended for the service of mankind, but for potential destructive use. This further muddles the vibratory nexus of your social memory complex, causing a situation where neither those oriented towards serving others nor those oriented towards serving self can gain the energy/power which opens the gates to intelligent infinity for the social memory complex (people with a veil of forgetting). This in turn causes the harvest to be small.

The military (third density entities) have bases undersea in the southern waters near the Bahamas, in Pacific seas close to Chilean borders on the water, on the moon (which is a satellite), in the skies, on the lands are very numerous and potentially destructive.

They came from the same place as humanity on Earth or Ra on Venus, they came from the Creator. On a shallower aspect, these people your other selves' government (national security).

The United States learned this technology from Nikola Tesla. When Nikola Tesla departed this illusion, the papers containing the necessary understanding were taken by mind/body/spirit complexes serving your security of national divisional complex. These people became privy (private information) to the basic technology. The technology was given to the Russians from the Confederation, about 27 years ago Ra states in 1954, in an attempt to share information and bring about peace among your peoples. The entities giving this information were in error, but Ra did many things in attempts to aid our harvest, where Ra learned the folly of certain types of aid. That is why Ra's approach is more cautious now, even as the need is power upon power greater, and our people's call is greater and greater.

The man-made UFO crafts from Tesla's technology are considered and used as weaponry today. The energy used is from the field of electromagnetic energy which polarizes the Earth sphere. The weaponry is of two basic kinds: psychotronic and particle beam. The weapons have been used to alter weather patterns and to enable the vibratory change which engulfs this planet at this time.

The governments of each of our societal-division desire to refrain from publicity in case of hostile action from any potential enemies.

The United States has 573 of these crafts in 1981 and was in the process of adding to this number, with the maximum speed being equal to the earth energy squared. This field varies. The limit is approximately half the light speed, due to imperfections in design.

Humanity on Earth possess technology capable of resolving each and every limitation which plagues our Social Memory Complex. The concerns some people on Earth have with powerful energy cause the solutions to be withheld until the solutions are so needed that those with the distortion can then become further distorted in the direction of power.

The Orion's landed here and their purpose is conquest, unlike those of the Confederation (positive density) who wait for the calling (the calling such as people's prayers or cry for help). The Orion group is of negative density calls itself to conquest. One form of landing is when the Orion's land, they take people on their craft and program them for future use. The first level of programing will be discovered by those who do research. The second, a triggering program. Third, a second and most deep triggering program crystallizing the entity, thereby rendering (making) it lifeless and useful as a kind of beacon.

The second form is a landing beneath the earth's crust, which is entered from water. This is the general area of your South American and Caribbean areas and close to the northern pole. The bases of these people are underground.

There are approximately 1,500 people, and growing, that know about the 573 crafts that the United States possessed in 1981, and most likely to this day still possess and perhaps even more.

These crafts are constructed one by one in the desert or Arid regions of New Mexico and Mexico, both installations being underground. Ra watches these developments and hopes our people on Earth may be harvested into 4th density in peace. People can not ride in them for they are controlled by computers from a remote source of data with no people inside. The United States and Mexico arranged for an underground installation of UFO craft in Mexico because of Mexico's ground being dry and near-total lack of population. The government officials who agreed did not know the use their land in Mexico would be put, but thought it was governmental research installation for bacteriological warfare. The approximate diameter being 23 feet.

Daniel Frye was transported, in thought-form, by the Confederation in order to give this mind/body/spirit complex data so that we might see how this type of contact aided your people in the uncovering of the Intelligent Infinity behind the illusion of your limits.

Episode 105: Wanderers frequently share characteristics exhibiting physical ailments such as allergies and personality disorders, which seem to be a reaction against this planet's vibrational frequency. This is apparently a side effect that is due to having another planetary influence in higher densities as their home vibration. They incarnate on this third-density planet in order to be of service in whatever way possible to help the population of this planet to become more aware of the evolutionary process and to move in harmony with it. These Wanderers go through the same forgetting process that every 3rd density being- even as they slowly begin to remember why it is that they have been born here. Apparently, about one in every 70 people on Earth is of such origin.

As we let love flow through us, others change, and as they open their hearts, the circle of light grows. We are now at a stage where light sources are beginning to connect (the global mind). This global mind happening faster with email and the World Wide Web. With information being exchanged without pen and paper, we are basically working with light. A great service is to know your worthiness and be yourself.

All beings can use discernment within the all-self, located at the heart of each entity.

The Confederation contacted Don's group in 1962 without spacecraft, but through thought-form.

The programming on the constructs of Men in Black makes it difficult to control them. People would not be able to grapple with a thought-form entity of the Men in Black.

There are no mistakes under the Law of One.

Ra: "The self-healing distortion is affected through realization of the Intelligent Infinity resting within. This is blocked in some way in those who are not perfectly balanced in bodily complexes. The blockages vary from entity to entity. It requires the conscious awareness of the spiritual nature of reality, if you will, and the corresponding pourings of this reality into the individual mind/body/spirit complex for healing to take place."

All three in the channeling group (Don Elkins, Carla, and Jim) with Ra are Wanderers of 5th and 6th density.

There are apparently many, many different ways people may receive such subconscious confirmations of the appropriateness of their thoughts or actions. The most common is the feeling of rightness that wells up from within when one is on the right track or receiving spiritually helpful information. These signs being synchronicities.

Sometimes silver flecks would end up on the groups faces or various places, this is a synchronistic sign indicating the appropriateness or importance of that learn/teaching (They learned it and then taught it). The entity itself, in cooperation with the inner planes, creates whatever signpost is most understandable or noticeable to it. Entities consciously do not create them. The roots of mind complex, having touched in understanding, Intelligent Infinity, creates them.

Before each contact with Ra, the group conducted a meditation that was used as our tuning device. The meditation was their means of becoming as one in their seeking to be of service to others.

Kathryn: "I was also told in a channeling session to meditate more, so I can further evolve. Another channeling session stated that a third density sign is fear or anxiety."

The desire that had brought Ra to our group (Don's channeling group) was a true desire for non-transient material, and this desire fueled their sessions. (Non-transient material is information aligned with the Law of One, as Ra would answer any question, but preferred the questions to align with the Law of One.)

Kathryn: "I'm glad Ra desired that because this information was much needed for humanity and has changed my life for the better and raised my positive polarity substantially to about 25% higher within 9 months."

Anything measurable is transient. Ra would remind the group to get back on track in a subtle way: by telling the group to watch their alignments. Later, they figured out that Ra was grading their questions, not the Bible near Carla's head as she was laying down nor their candle placement.

The human spirit, the force of creative love, the creation's essence: these things are unfindable, noumenal (knowledge that exists independent of human senses), it's always sensed, and never penetrated by our fact-finding intellects. But we sense into them through living with an open heart, and by talking about them with sources such as Ra and Q'uo and other "universal or "outer" energies and essences. The personal guides and other teachers of the inner planes of our planet have much more leeway in offering personal information. People can go to them to get readings on health and other specific issues. People can go to outer sources such as our Confederation sources with questions that transcend space time. If it will matter less in 10,000 years than it does not, it is probably not a universal question for Ra.

Episode 106: The crater found in Russia in the Tunguska region was caused by the destruction of a fission reactor. This was a "drone" sent by the Confederation, which malfunctioned. It was moved to an area where its destruction would not cause infringement upon the will of mind/body/spirit complexes. It was then detonated.

Its purpose in coming to Earth: It as a drone designed to listen to the various signals of people on Earth. People were at that time, beginning to work in a more technical sphere. The Confederation was interested in determining the extent and the rapidity of our advances. The drone was powered by a simple fission motor or engine. It was not that type which you now know, but was very small. However, it has the same destructive effect upon third-density molecular structure. Thus, as it malfunctioned, the

Confederation and Ra felt it was best to pick a place for its destruction rather than attempt to retrieve it, for the possibility/probability modes for this maneuver, looked very, very minute.

There was very little radiation in this type of device. There is radiation which is localized, but the localization does not drift with the winds as does the emission of our somewhat primitive weapons. There's very little radiation in the trees in the area. This is an example of radiation being very localized. However, the energy which is released is powerful enough to cause difficulties.

Nuclear power was brought through by a basic equation from Albert, a Wanderer, dedicated to service the planet. This work was not given by higher densities nor intended for destruction.

The phenomenon known as spontaneous combustion of human beings is a random occurrence which does not have to do with the entity. They are random entities. One tree being struck by lightning and burning, but lightning not striking elsewhere, therefore, elsewhere not burning, is an example of the random occurrence.

Episode 107: Ra innocently "told on" Carla about a good friend of hers offering her the opportunity to experience the effects of LSD, which she had never experienced before. She used it twice in early February 1981 as a programming device to attempt to achieve an experience of unity with Creator, but she did not wish Don to know about these experiences, since he was very much against the use of any illegal substances at any time and especially while working with Ra.

In a later session it will be suggested by Ra that these two experiences were arranged by the negative entities monitoring the groups work with those of Ra, in hopes that Carla's ability to serve in the Ra contact might be hindered. The three of them then determined there would be no further use of any illegal substances for as long as they were privileged to work with the Ra contact, so that no chinks in their "armor of light" that they could eliminate would be present, and so that the Ra contact could never be associated with the use of any such drugs.

The information on Aleister Crowley is self-explanatory and underlines again the caution that each seeker must take in moving carefully through its energy canters in a balanced fashion. So, one could carefully balance the energy centers and not use drugs for assistance.

Carla and Don were together, wed in spirit, but Don didn't want marriage and wanted 'to stay celibate. After two years Carla knew celibacy wasn't for her but was still in love with Don. She then had lovers and would tell Don before it started and when she stopped seeing them. Don was gone flying as a pilot half the time, so Carla found time for lovers. Her lover 10 of the 16 years she spent with Don was a trusted and much-loved friend of hers ever since High School. He came and saw her about once a month. She then stopped seeing him when he wanted to take the relationship further, and then she was celibate for 4 years before Jim (the scribe of the Law of One material). Carla believed that the weakness in Don's armor of light that resulted in his dying was believing Carla fell out of love for him and Don doubted her allegiance to him. He never told her this and she thought he was happy for her. For six years she had suicidal thoughts after Don's death.

Jim and Carla eventually got married three years after Don's death. Ra said in the density her and Don came from; they were already one. Carla then believed her and Jim's relationship was "child's play". All three of them loved each other and worked well together.

The Confederations teachings are at one with universal wisdom as well as living in love. Carla said, "That focus upon Love is one's access to truth, and one's willingness to keep the heart open, which one may call faith, is the energy that brings to us all that was meant for us, both of lessons to learn and of service to offer."

Ra tried to express the feeling of the infinite mystery of the one creation in its infinite and intelligent unity.

Sexual intercourse was an aid to Carla's vital energies during the trance state and would increase the length of a session if engaged in the night before a session was to be held. Thus, at the end of session 18 of 106, when Don asked how they might avoid further difficulties in the contact (such as not taking LSD) Ra affirmed the aid they had discovered was that of the sexual intercourse. They also found that conscious dedication of the act of love-making to the service of others via the Ra contact increased its beneficial effects.

Ra further states that there are substances ingested, such as LSD or Marijuana, that do aid the individual in the positive service it has chosen. This is due to the distortion towards chemical lapses within the mind complex, causing lack of synaptic continuity. This is a chemical reaction of short duration. The instrument, Carla, however, has not used this particular substance at any time while performing extent due to the energizing or speeding up of the vital forces. However, it is not recommended for the instrument due to the toll it takes upon the vital energies once the substance wears off. This being true of any speeding-up chemical.

The prerequisite of the contact for those involved is the tuning in the personal life and meditation before each contact: Including contemplation, or prayer before entering these workings. Ra stated certain people wanting to join the Ra contact circle weren't of proper vibrational distortion. (Perhaps the lack of simple faith he had, since he wanted to prove spiritual truth.)

Ra felt the primary importance in personal ethics is allowing people to do their own learning, make their own mistakes, cannot be over emphasized.

Episode 108: The prayer of St. Francis is what Carla used in her own personal tuning mechanism since she began channeling in 1974. It further refines the tuning done by the support group and is always grayed mentally before any session, whether telepathic or trance.

The limitations of which Ra speaks refer to Carla's rheumatoid arthritis, which was apparently chosen before the incarnation to provide an inner focus for her meditative work rather than to allow the ease of outer expression that might have dissipated the inner orientation. Thus, not all disabilities are meant to yield to even the best efforts of healers, and when such a disability does not respond to any kind of healing effort, one may begin to consider what opportunities for learning and service are opened up by the disability. Ra even mentioned that her acceptance of her disabilities and limitations would ease the amount of pain that she suffered because of them.

Kathryn: "I also feel that I chose to have a great BMX life by exploring, traveling the United States racing, having a lot of friends and acquaintances and enjoy being in the physical outer world. Then, chose before birth that at some point in my life to have some sort of limitation when I broke my neck at 25 years old in 2015. Immediately I knew I would write a book by April of 2015, this unfortunately is when the channeler of the Ra contact, Carla Reuckert passed away. During this month I had a spinal fusion of the skull to C5.

Upon publishing my book, I began having vivid dreams about the future because of my desire to serve others. After publishing my 2nd book, I began manifesting money and began investing. I then would share my dreams of the future on YouTube and consistently started having more of these dreams after publishing each one online. The book was an action I took and the universe saw that as a service to humanity and therefore more manifestation came into my life, as well as dreams.

Next, when I learned about the Law of One, the dreams became more detailed, accurate, vivid and even would show me some Law of One concepts such as when I had the "I am One" dream about each person having a higher self that guides us throughout our life. I am the most accurate prophet or dream interpreter in the world, whereas every Christian so-called prophet had at least one wrong. To their religion that would mean they would be considered a false prophet.

I definitely believe my inner focus, spiritual transformation, my books, the 33 accurate dreams of the future fulfilled, 14 years of research in various topics and now my studies on the Law of One is because I am now forced to be off the bike and thus, discovered everything I have over these past 10 years learning everything I can about discovering the truth of this world and the universe. If seven years is like obtaining a masters degree and the Law of One books is like a PhD study in metaphysics; then this would be my PhD thesis."

Why Carla, the channeler, would smell incense at various times during the day at various places: This instrument has spent a lifetime in dedication to service. This has brought this instrument to this nexus in space/time with the conscious and unconscious distortions toward service, with the further conscious distortion towards service by communication. Each time they perform the working, Ra's social memory complex vibrational distortion meshes more firmly with Carla's unconscious distortions towards service. Thus, Ra is becoming a part of Carla's vibratory complex, and a vice versa. This occurs upon the unconscious level, the level where the mind has gone down through to the roots of consciousness called cosmic. Carla isn't consciously aware of the slow changing of the meshing vibratory complex. However, as the dedications on both levels continues, and the workings continue, there are signals sent from the unconscious in a symbolic manner. Carla is extremely keen in her sense of smell, it takes place unconsciously, and the thought-form of this odor is witnessed by the entity.

Carla felt better and healthier because of the channeling sessions. This is because for many years she prayed before communication with Ra. Then, before the trance state was achieved, the prayer remained within the conscious portion of the mind. This wasn't as effective as the vibrational sound then goes into the unconscious level, thus affecting the communication from the spiritual complex. Also, her accepting certain limitations which it placed upon itself in order to serve such as she does now. This also is an aid to realigning the distortions of physical pain.

Episode 109: Henry Puharich wasn't involved in the channelings because he wasn't of proper vibrational distortion due to him wanting to prove spiritual truth instead of just having simple "faith".

The movie Battle beyond the Star had some distortions of the Law of One and its scenario upon our physical plane (Earth).

UFOs are certainly here; the landing-trace cases alone prove that something that makes dents in the ground is visiting us, and the many witnesses and abductees create a comprehensive picture of human alien contact that is undeniable.

Did Dwight Eisenhower meet with the Confederation or Orion group in 1950s? Dwight Eisenhower met with thought-forms indistinguishable from third density. This was a test, the Confederation wanted to see what would occur if this extremely positively-oriented and simple (pleasant) person with no significant distortion towards power happened across peaceful information. The Confederation and Ra discovered that Eisenhower did not feel those under his care could deal with the concepts of other beings and other philosophies.

Thus, an agreement reached then would allow him to go his way and the Confederation to do likewise- and a very quiet campaign be continued alerting people on Earth to the Confederations presence gradually, events have overtaken this plan such as witnesses seeing UFOs and so forth.

Ra didn't want to infringe upon our future but gave hints that a crashed spaceship with small bodies inside now may be stored in our military installations.

Negative entities performing psychic attacks/greetings can be looked upon in a negative way, therefore, having a negative experience; one can also choose to see the Creator in all entities and events and can praise and seek the light within any situation.

When the latter choice is made, the psychic greeting becomes a great blessing for this presents an intensive opportunity to see the One Creator where it may be more difficult to see. When accomplished, develops a great deal more spiritual strength than may normally be developed without the negative entities aid in pointing out the weaker areas. Our poor choices, usually reflecting a lack of love toward another self, get magnified by the demon and bleed away our efforts to seek the light and serve others until we are able to show love, acceptance, compassion, tolerance and light tough to all. This is why Jesus said to "resist no evil." To resist and fight is to see someone or something as other than the self, as other than the One Creator. This is the negative path. The positive path sees and loves all as the self and as the One.

Carla's cold chest is from taking LSD. The chemical substance has within it the facility of removing large stores of energy. This was carefully planned by the negative being (Orion's) not wanting Carla to remain viable. The first hope of the Orion entity which arranged this opportunity was that Carla would become less polarized towards the positive.

Due to conscious efforts upon Carla, using the substance as a programmer for service to others and for thankfulness, Carla was spared this distortion and there was no result satisfactory to the Orion group. Carla is a very strong entity with very little distortions from universal green-ray love energy. Thus, the negative 5th density beings plan was not affected, as Carla continued to give of itself an open or green-ray manner rather than attempting to deceive or manipulate other-selves.

Since Carla wouldn't cease in sharing love universally under this substance, the negative beings only remaining distortion available was to drain this entity of as much energy as possible. Busyness is not the appropriate attitude for this work, which Carla is trying to overcome.

LSD caused Carla to become busy and lack the derive to rest; Carla staying alert for much longer than appropriate created vital energy to be lost. Making her unusually susceptible to infections, such as the cold chest.

How to best revitalize the self? Meditation, accepting of limitations, experiences of joy through association with others, singing, exercising with great contact whenever possible, with the life forces of second density, especially those of trees; also, be aware of moderate intake of food, exercise suggested at a fairly early portion of the day and at a later portion of the day before resting was given to Carla (the channeler).

The first LSD debilitating effects is approximately 3 days. The 2nd ingestion has a cumulative or doubling effect.

Episode 110: The first working with Confederation entities was with Atlantis approximately 13,000 years ago. Paul Shockley received information, while channeling the Confederation that he took part in the design and construction of the Egyptian pyramids. This memory was integrated into the service of healing and polarization possible by mechanisms of the crystal and the charged healer.

Paul's second experience was approximately 12,000 years ago, during which the entity prepared, in some part, the consciousness of people in Egypt to enable the calling that enabled those of Ra's social memory complex to walk among the Egyptians at the time. He was a priest and succeeded in remembering in semi-distorted form the learn/teachings of the Atlantean pyramidal experiences. Thus became a builder of the archetypal thought of the Law of One with distortions towards healing, which aided Ra in bringing this through into physical manifestation.

There were other beings aiding in the construction of the pyramids, but not fully materialized in third density. They were materialized from their waste up to their heads but not from their waist to their feet.

Intelligent Infinity present in the absorption of livingness and beingness as it becomes codified into intelligent energy, due to thought impression of those assisting the living stone into a new shape of beingness. The release and use of Intelligent Infinity for a brief period begins to absorb all the consecutive or interlocking dimensions, thus offering brief glimpses of those projecting to material their thoughts. These beings beginning to materialize but not remaining visible. Those beings were the thought-form of Ra's social memory complex as they offered contact from their intelligent infinity to the intelligent infinity of the stone.

Carla was told that she has experience in healing on levels other than the physical. She was told to never practice the exercise of fire, as it is used in a stronger form of healing. She was advised by Ra never to do any kind of physical healing on others, because she was always very low on physical energy, and such healing would tend to drain her already low reserve in that area. This is to conserve her vital energies during a three-month period.

Since she was a child, she had some sort of ability to sit with someone with hands in contact and be able to clear some of the surface clutter away from the other person's mind or being. She can also do spiritual balancing by her hands.

Could a machine from Washington State being developed that was suppose to augment the general health and well-being of a person aid Carla? Ra's response suggested that Carla's magnetic field was somewhat unusual and very likely formed in such an unusual way as to permit contact with those of Ra. This unusual magnetic field has been a source of frequent inconveniences with any electromagnetic equipment that Carla has used on a regular basis. She breaks it- just by touching it periodically. She can't wear anything, but quarts crystal watches, and the channeling group has many, many semi-functional tape recorders lying around different areas of the house.

(Judgement ceases when we choose to view all as the Creator. There's no room for judgement, but the observation of a individualized portion of consciousness of the Creator.)

Ra says there are no mistakes. I'd like to add that we are all just learning and growing at different rates, so there's no mistakes since we are all just learning.

Episode 111: How to have Protection Against Negative entities? Protection lies in giving thanksgiving for each moment and experience. See yourself and others as the Creator. Open your heart and always know the light and praise it.

Carla's physical energy level was always very low and constantly being drained by arthritis and pain, so she had to engage in daily exercise in order to maintain the function of each portion of her body. (I believe exercise is why I don't have neck or back pain after breaking my neck and having surgery.)

For Carla- She walked rapidly for about an hour a day.

Jim McCarthy: "One way of looking at the process of evolution is to see it as the process of solving the mysteries all about us. All events are illusions or mysteries because each represents the One Creator in one disguise of another, offering us a greater or lesser opportunity to find love, joy, balance and perfection in each moment.

During the three-month period Ra suggests Carla should achieve intensification in her workout by doing one long one instead of two shorter ones. Ra stated she needs the strengthening of the body. This may be one major exercise period and then one more half the length at night before meditation. Ra, "This will be seen to be wearing upon the instrument. However, it will have the effect of strengthening the physical complex and lessening the vulnerability which might be taken advantage of."

Episode 112: Any third density entity has a Higher Self or Oversoul at mid-sixth density. In addition, Wanderers who are a member of a social memory complex also has another complex of consciousness upon which to call for assistance.

The forgetting process, or the veil, occurs when we take on flesh and become a manifested entity on Earth, that flesh shuts our metaphysical senses. All that we knew before birth is hidden in the deeper mind. There is always the fear, especially among Wanderers, as one enters incarnation, that one will not awaken at all but be lost for the whole life experience.

The awakening process beings to identify with a new and larger concept of the self as an eternal and metaphysical being.

As we all awaken and develop our truer selves, we can help each other. People will come your way. They seem very "aware" or very confused or scared. If the Creator put them in your way, then you are well equipped to aid them. Simply love and accept them, as well as show this truth of the Law of One if you so desire. This involves first coming to love and accept yourself, forgiving yourself and forgive others. For judgement of others stops when we view others and ourself as the One Creator. (A fractal of God perhaps).

Qualification for contact with Ra includes penetrating the forgetting process. Otherwise, the Law of confusion/Free will would prohibit this.

How to disseminate information to be of service to others?

Ra: "Relax, and let the Law of Attraction work. Even if only one person is aided by the work, that is enough. At the very least, the benefit that the material provides to the group alone will become like unto a light that each in the group will radiate to all others met in the daily round of activities."

Kathryn's channeling: "Some people are told they must sacrifice in order to serve, but the truth is that it is well to make sure your own needs and desires are met first before serving. Sacrificing is a form of martyrdom that once wisdom is utilized one may realize they don't need to sacrifice and can meet their own needs first before fully serving others."

My search for truth began after breaking my neck BMX racing at 25-years old. I knew at that time I was meant to start writing books, do research and search for truth in every area of life. To ultimately master this density on Earth. I chose to work at "boring" jobs according to some people in order to get all this research in. Therefore, I essentially was doing this full time and being paid for it. I was always right where I was supposed to be. After 10 years of consistent full-time research, it finally took off and I wrote these seven books in the first half of 2024, two of them were already finished, but just needed to be edited.

I knew the exact 10 books I needed to read and questions I needed to channel in or to solve the entire puzzle of how this world and our universe works. It's here in these five *Law of One* books as well as my book called *"Correcting Distortions of the Bible."* The answers the whole world has been looking for is finally here. This was my purpose and perhaps my PhD study, as well as the reason I chose to reincarnate into Earth at this time."

Ra said to not be concerned with how many people get this information. They are content with being able to aid in the evolution of one of our people's here on Earth. Whatever effort the group makes cannot disappoint Ra, for that number already exceeds one.

The Ra contact was very wearing on Carla as she would lose 2-3 pounds per session and the negative beings wanting to attack, so that this information wouldn't get out into the public. This often intensified her pain of her arthritic distortions to the point that her function on all levels was severely curtailed. Carla was very happy to serve in this way and to see Don happy and inspired during the contact was satisfaction to Carla that struck the depths of her being. Donald was her world. She adored him and wish to make him comfortable and happy. But he was not comfortable in this world and so often lonely and isolated. The days of Ra contact were golden for Don and Carla and she would have died quite gladly doing one last session to be of service, and even expected to, but Don's death came first when he took his own life. (Perhaps his unhappiness was due to Carla having Jim as a lover, but Don wouldn't fulfill her desires because of his celibacy. Thus, something like this is to be expected I would assume. She even waited four years being celibate with Don and he still wouldn't meet her desires in that way.

Carla hopes that her life is to remain simply the giving of all she has to the Creator. That's why Jesus said "If you gave to the least of these you've given to me." Because Jesus, you, me and even the least of these is the Creator.

Carla found life a wonder and a joy, and all the limitations, mess, loss and pain in the world have not changed her mind on that.

The demons tend to want to attack Wanderers more than those people who haven't come from higher densities into Earth's 3rd density life to help humanity. Thus, Ra stated that the demons were doing everything they could to undermine Carla at this time, such as her experiencing a problem with her foot so that she couldn't exercise. Ra stated that it is fortunate that she be greatly involved in worship of the One Infinite Creator through sacred song during this time. Ra said the more physical active movements of exercise and in the sexual sense are helpful. Again, it is fortunate that this instrument has the opportunities for loving social intercourse, which are of some substantial benefit.

During meditation, Don once saw a world where the colors were three-dimensional. He saw living waters, and a golden sunrise streaming over the sky. The 3D colors made our sunrise streaming over the sky; and they made our earthly hues look like black-and-white photos. Another experience was Don's lower arm moving rapidly up and down while rested on the arm chair and a blue light emanating from his lower arm. Later transmissions indicating that UFO entities were winding his batteries.

Ra stated that these experiences would best be approached from ceremonial magic stance. However, the Wanderer or adept shall have the far-greater potential for this type of experience, which is an archetypal nature, one belonging to the roots of consciousness. ((Perhaps obtaining Christ Consciousness of 4th density or above.)) His experience was a form of initiation.

Ra states that it is not well for positively oriented entities to work alone.

A strong desire to be of service is not enough when not combined with wisdom. The group suffered in the first months of the Ra contact from doing too many sessions. For example, scheduling too many sessions in such a short period of time was overly draining on Carla's physical energy especially after she had consumed LSD. This shortened energy meant that the total number of sessions that was possible during her incarnation was probably being reduced. (Perhaps a good balance of rest and service is well.)

The power of dedication- If Carla dedicated herself to having a session with Ra, she would expend an amount of energy equal to a full day's work- even if the session did not occur. Thus, it was most important for dedication to be met with wisdom, such as not overdoing it.

Ra says martyrdom is not necessarily helpful. ((Complete unconditional love in service-to-others should be met with wisdom. Perhaps the perfect balance of service-to-others and wisdom. An example of this is Carla having the wisdom to take enough rest so that she'll have enough energy to do more sessions. Thus, the wisdom allowing more service-to-others to be done.

The tone in Don's left ear when starting the communication with Ra was a negatively oriented signal trying to interfere with the group's communication with Ra. A positively oriented signal would be in the right ear indicating a sign that one is being given some unworded saying, such as, "Listen, Take heed." The other positive sign is the tone above the head, which is a balanced confirmation of a thought.

We are all things so we can get a negative signal in receiving thought-forms, word-forms and visions. Thought-forms, word-forms and visions can also be positively oriented as well.

Carla's energy was lost just by her dedication to the service of others through the Ra contact, so even if they stopped the session early, that energy would already be lost as if she did a full and complete session.

Thus, once vital energy is dedicated by the instrument to Ra's communications, even if the working did not occur, this vital energy would be last to the day-to-day experience of the instrument. Ra indicated the importance of releasing the will from determining the times of working, for if the instrument desires contact, the energy is gathered and lost for ordinary or mundane purposes. Therefore, the group decided to continue the session since the energy was already lost. Carla's determination to continue contact during that period has already extended the low-energy period.

In order to nullify negatively oriented signals, dreams and clairaudient communication, the group must share the negatively oriented experiences with the group and meditate in love. One must not downgrade the experiences or it'll invite the prolonging of the effects. It's for the better to share and trust such experiences and join hearts and souls in love and light with compassion for the sender and armor for the self.

Carla had a dream of Orion (negative) influence. The essence of the dream revealing more the instruments unconscious associative patterns of symbolism.

Don's arm glowing blue and moving rapidly involuntarily was an analogy from his Higher Self that the being that he was living in, in a way is not understood by physicists, scientists or doctors.

His experience was his ability to contact intelligent Infinity during meditation. Therefore, it doesn't have a direct effect upon Carla's vital energy.

To aid oneself in vital energy is to be sensitive to beauty, to singing of sacred music, to mediation and worship, to the sharing of self with others in freely given love either in social or sexual intercourse. These things work directly upon vitality. Appreciating a variety of experiences is a less direct way that aids vitality.

The diagram of the advancement of magical practices, starting with Malkuth, Yesod, Hod, Netzach, Tiphareth ect. Ending in Kether each has a complex number and shading of energy centers, as well as some part in various balances; the lower, the middle, the high, and the total balance. Thus, there are complex colors or rays and complex charges in each station. These stations are relationships. Each path, positive or negative, has these relationships offered. The intent of the practitioner in working with these powerful concepts determines the polarity of the working. The tools are tools.

The Ipsissimus is one who has mastered the tree of Life and has used his mastery for negative polarization.

There was a quite significant probability of Carla developing pulmonary or renal disease in session 44 around April of 1981. The group averted a possible serious physical malfunction of Carla's body. Their prayerful support was helpful, just as Carla's unflagging determination to accept what is best in the long run and maintain the recommended exercises without impatience. She is also aided by rest and the balancing with exercise.

A significant portion of Ra's Social Memory Complex are sixth-density Wanderers here on Earth. Another large portion of Ra consists of those who aided those in South America, where 150 became harvestable for graduation into 4th density 50,000 years ago after the first 25,000-year cycle (here on Earth). Earth is now in the third 25,000-year cycle, close to the 75,000-year cycle of 3rd density. Therefore, Earth is close to the graduation of souls from this density into the 4th. 65% of souls on Earth are currently of positive polarity. Another portion of Ra are those aiding Atlantis. All are sixth density and all brother and sister groups due to the unified feeling that Ra had been aided by the pyramids, so they could aid people on Earth.

Two people in the group are of sixth-density origin, one a fifth density harvestable to sixth but choosing to return as a Wanderer due to loving association between teach and student. Thus, the three form a greatly cohesive group.

Kathryn: "My guess is that since Carla and Don are one in a higher-density and in love with each other, they are of 6th density and Jim must then be of 5th density origin."

The spiritual transfer of energy, is possible for Carla in any sexual-energy transfer. It happens without any particular effort on her part and seems due to her nature of how she may be of service to another. This kind of spiritual-energy transfer is possible for anyone to achieve through the dedication of shared sexual intercourse for the purpose of achieving such a transfer.

With that dedication consciously made, the male will transfer the physical energy, which he has in abundance, to the female and refresh her. And the female will transfer the mental/emotional and spiritual energies, which she has in abundance, and inspire the male. The biological male tends to express the male principle of that quality that reaches. The biological female tends to express the female principle of awaiting the reaching. The orgasm, of either positively oriented entity, is the point the transfer takes place, although well-mated partners do not need to experience the orgasm in order to achieve the transfer.

The energy transfer from James McCarty gave Carla the vital energy needed to still be alive after she ran out of energy some years ago, essentially the sexual energy transfer from Jim saved Carla's life.

With that dedication consciously made, the male will transfer the physical energy, which he has in abundance, to the female and refresh her. And the female will transfer the mental/emotional and spiritual energies, which she has in abundance, and inspire the male.

With proper balance of mind and body, the orgasm can activate the spirit complex and serves as a kind of shuttle, to allow an entity to contact intelligent infinity.

Pioneer thinkers theorize that unblocking lower energy centers can in some degree activate the frontal lobes of the brain.

No one knows for sure what that part of the brain is for, but if activated can quantum leap in consciousness.

At 25 years old Jim started having frontal lobe experiences when waking up in the morning. It's a combination of pleasure and pressure which starts in the frontal lobes, then spreads and pulses through the whole brain, feeling like an orgasm in the brain. Often being accompanied by voices and visions. He had over 200 of those from 25-34. This may be experienced after a concentration of effort upon the opening of the gateway or indigo mind complex so that experience of a sacramental or violet ray may occur.

These experiences are the beginnings of the body, the mind and the spirit becoming integrated at the gateway or indigo level, they may then experience joy and the comprehension of intelligent infinity. Thus, the body complex orgasm and mind complex orgasm becoming integrated may then set forth the proper gateway for the spiritual-complex integration and its use as a shuttle for the sacrament of the fully experienced presence of the one Infinite Creator.

Each person has several guides available to it. The persona of two of these guides is the polarity of male and female. The third is androgynous and represents a more unified conceptualization faculty.

When Carla and Don were small kids, they both saw a ball of lightning. The ball of lightning came in through Carla's window rolled around her crib, and left through the same window. (When I was 30 years old in 2019, I saw a ball of lightning go through my window as well and then through the doorway into the hallway. It occurred right after my family had prayed over the house.) Ra said Carla was being visited by her people to be wished well.

Some entities feel the need to plant Confederation imagery in a way not to interfere with free will. So, they use symbols of death, resurrection, love and peace as a means of creating upon the thought level, the systematic train of events which give the message of hope and love.

This type of contact is chosen by the careful consideration of Confederation members which contact an entity of like home vibration. This project then goes before the Council of Saturn and, if approved, is completed. This type of contact includes the nonpainful nature of thought experienced and the message content which speaks of the new dawning age and not of doom.

Ra encourages us to balance faults and not erase them. Of course, if one has a fault that involves infringing on the free will of another, then the fault does need to be addressed by eliminating that behavior or you can polarize more negative. One does not find ways to balance stealing or murder. But anger, vagueness and forgetfulness and people's little quirks can be balanced and not removed.

Kathryn: "One day when I almost tried judging someone, I remembered they are part of the Creator and the judgement disappeared. We are all on different levels of evolution, so there's no need to judge, for all eventually returns to the Creator anyways. We all evolve positively in the sixth and once in the seventh density upon graduation we will go into the next octave of Creation, in the new universe."

The work of sixth density is to unify wisdom and compassion. This entity, Jim, abounds in wisdom. The compassion it is desirous of balancing has, as its antithesis, lack of compassion. In the more conscious being, this expresses or manifests itself as lack of compassion for the self.

Carla's pre-incarnation to choose to have arthritis was, so that she could focus on her inner life of meditation and contemplation, instead of the usual activities of the world. Such pre-incarnatively chosen limitations confound many healers, who have the opinion that no disease is ever necessary. However, it seems that some people choose limitations that will utilize the entire incarnation and not just a portion of it.

(Perhaps Carla channeling could have been because of her limitations and maybe if she didn't have limitations, then her life would have taken her somewhere else and millions of people would not have been blessed to receive this information of *The Law of One*. Then, my limitations coming at 25 years old after breaking my neck, further confirms this because I know if I never broke my neck, I most likely would still be racing bikes instead of my 10 years of research, writing my seventh book right now and condensing this much needed material so many others could easily obtain this information for their evolution. These distortions present opportunities not meant for healing efforts.)

Carla had a love for Jesus and promised to give praise, thanksgiving and glory to his name and to share her story as a Wanderer coming from the 6th density to 3rd density Earth to be of service. She couldn't wait to do another Ra session, just to see how happy it would make Don. It seemed to be the only time she did see him happy was when these sessions were going on. Don felt Carla's best chance for healing was in mental work at his Church of Christ Scientist mother's faith. When someone had a cold or illness the practitioner was called, who would spend time in prayer and meditation, affirming the perfection of whatever seemed to be imperfect.

Carla felt she lacked compassion to balance wisdom, so she chose an incarnative experience to develop compassion by being placed in situations of accepting self in the absence of others acceptance and their acceptance without expecting a return or energy transfer. Ra said, "This is not an easy program for an incarnation but was deemed proper by this entity. This entity therefore must need to meditate and consciously, moment by moment, accept the self in its limitations, which have been placed for the very purpose of bringing this entity to the precise tuning we are using. Further, having learned to radiate acceptance and love without expecting return, this entity now must balance this by learning to accept the gifts of love and acceptance of others which this instrument feels some discomfort in accepting. These two balanced workings will aid this entity in the release from the distortion of pain. The limitations are, to a great extent, fixed."

As a child, Carla always wanted to be of service but unable to fit well anywhere, she felt so sure she'd never be able to be of service she prayed that she might die at 13. (Six months after trying to take her life, the negative beings went after her kidney until kidney failure and she experienced a near death experience. During this near-death experience she was told that she could go on if she chose to, but that her work was not done. She immediately chose to return to this life, now feeling that there was indeed service to be provided, and the juvenile rheumatoid arthritis set in immediately.)

Carla's desire to leave this density lowered the defenses of an already predisposed weak body, and an allergic reaction was so intensified as to cause the complications which distorted the body towards unviability. The will of Carla, when she found that there was indeed work to be done in service, was again the guiding factor or complex of vibratory patterns which kept the body complex from surrendering to dissolution that cause the vitality of life.

Ra said war, catastrophe, weather changes and famine is a possible condition that would be greatly spread across the surface of the globe than anything Earth has experienced in the past, and therefore touch a larger percentage of the population in this form of catalyst.

There are those now experimenting with one of the major weapons in 1981 of this scenario, that is, the so-called psychotronic group of devices which are being experimentally used to cause such alterations in wind and weather as will result in eventual famine. If this program is not countered and proves experimentally satisfactory, the methods in this scenario would be made public. There would then be Russians that hope to be a bloodless invasion of their personnel in this and every land deemed valuable. However, the people of Earth have little propensity (proneness) for bloodless surrender.

Ra said there's nothing the group could do to seek aid from the Confederation in order to alleviate Carla's physical problems. (I would assume this to be that preincarnatively she chose to have this condition in order to carry out this information of *The Law of One* someday. Just like I believe I must have chosen to break my neck one day, so that I was then forced to go inwards that would eventually put me on the journey to where I am now of publishing these books.)

The most appropriate method to alleviate the physical problems: Exercise according to ability, not to exceed appropriate parameters, the nutrition, the social intercourse with companions, the sexual intercourse in greenway or above, (which is done in love and seeing them as the Creator.) and in general, the sharing of the distortions of this group's individual experiences in a helpful, loving manner.

Don and Jim were both loners and liked their own company and not much fond of society, although they were excellent hosts when company did come by, so they sacrificed their alone time, so the three of them can join together. The sacrifices were gladly made and the group felt very blessed to be together. When the Ra contact began three weeks later after all coming together as a group, they felt very happy that they had joined forces in faith. They had that clear, pure, unmuddied love and fellowship that stems from there being no fear between them, or needs that were not met. Carla believes that Don's decline and death were the result of his becoming fearful she might leave him for Jim, which Carla said she would have never done that. He never expressed the fear and Carla knew nothing of it until Don's friends said something months after the funeral about Don thinking Carla might have fallen out of love with him. Carla believes this led to his woeful last months, in which he suffered so greatly.

In 1968, Don and Carla wrote a book called The Crucifixion of Esmerelda Sweetwater after the commitment was made to work for the betterment of the planetary sphere, this commitment activated a possibility/probability vortex of some strength. The experience of generating this volume was unusual in that it was visualized as if watching a movie. Time had become available in its present moment form. The scenario of the volume went smoothly except the ending. They could not end the volume or visualize it due to free will. They wrote the book from what they saw under the influence of magnetic attraction which was released when the commitment was made and full memory of the dedication of this mission restored.

(Therefore, when they committed to work for the betterment of humanity it activated a possibility/probability (prophecy) of some strength, so they could write the book based on seeing the probability/possibility of the future, except they couldn't see the death due to free will. This played out in their own lives 13 years later in 1981 when they began channeling Ra. They couldn't see an ending in the story due to free will. Which later, Don in his own free will took his life corresponding to the death in the end of the book they wrote 13 years earlier.

During the Ra contact there was a misplacement of Carla, the instrument, under certain unprotected conditions, by the fifth-density negative entity that monitored the Ra sessions. This was unusual because Don and Carla wrote about an identical situation in the book The Crucifixion of Esmeralda Sweetwater 13 years earlier. The ending of the book they wrote seemed to be a symbolic description of Don's death in November 1984. Therefore, they saw possibilities into the future, wrote a book about it and it played out in their lives. (I also wrote a book of possible future events after the same commitment, as well as I had an injury that made me create content just like Carla did. These similarities are surprising.)

Ra knew the needed elements for communication with someone on Earth, which had any chance of the communication enduring. Ra could see a spectrograph of a complex paint sample and a complex of elements. So, Ra compared their color chip to many individuals and groups over a long span of time. Carla, Don and Jim's spectrograph matched their sample. So, the group was of appropriate vibrational frequency to be able to endure a long enough duration of communication with Ra.

Carla's ability to accept the limitations she placed on herself before birth delayed her 2nd surgery by four years. Her first surgery was upcoming in 1981 during the Ra contact. The arthritis in her hands set limitations more strongly than when the Ra contact began.

Ra said certain prayers from her Episcopalian Christian church and the communion service in particular were felt by Ra to be of aid to her. The Banishing Ritual of the Lesser Pentagram, which the group had used to purify their place before working with the Ra contact, was suggested for her hospital room and the operating room. The greatest protective and healing device was seen to be love. Any ritual such as prayer, communion, or the Banishing Ritual of the Lesser Pentagram actually alerts the positively polarized, discarnate entities so that they may provide that quality of love from their quarters, for whatever the purpose might be. The group may also provide love as a function of their truly caring for another. As they learn the lessons of love within the third density illusion, they are also learning the basics of healing and protection.

The spiritual/emotional complex, love, which is felt for Carla by Don and Jim, will be of aid whether this is expressed or unmanifest, as there is no protection greater than love.

Ra said it's not essential to purify a place, the power of visualization may aid in your support where you cannot intrude in your physical form. This means that the group can visualize the operating room and a visualization of the three of them performing the Banishing ritual in the room as they physically perform it in another location is one correct method of achieving their desired configuration.

The better method for those more practiced would be to leave the physical body and in the other body, enter the room and practice the ritual.

Can Carla meditate in the hospital without someone holding her hand? Ra suggested that Carla can pray with safety but only meditate with another entity's tactile (touchable) protection.

Carla can use warmed water moved gently over the physical vehicle while seated would be of some aid if practiced daily after exercising.

The exercise of fire performed before the session was of slight physical aid to Carla. This will increase as the practitioner learns/teaches its healing art. Carla was given vital energy due to the support she was given by Don and Jim.

Was the fire healing art properly done? Ra said the baton is well visualized. The conductor will learn to hear the entire score of the great music of its art. Carla must accept her limitations to create healing for herself. This is her preincarnative choice.

Ra mentioned a number of times that impatience is one of the most frequent catalysts with which the seeker must work on. When we see the path of evolution, we should be patient enough and not jump ahead the path quickly towards the goal.

Ra suggested to carefully place the foundation of one's house before hanging the roof.

Ra said in the context of doing work in the personality; in order to be more efficient in the central acceptance of the self, it is first necessary to know the distortions of the self that the entity is accepting. Each thought and action need to be scrutinized for the precise foundation of any reactions. This process shall lead to the more central task of acceptance. However, the architrave (the main beam of material resting across the columns of a building) must be in place before structure is built.

UFO contact reveals the general way in which many face-to-face encounters between people and extraterrestrial entities occur. What is actually remembered by the third-density entity is a product of its expectations and what the subconscious mind thinks is an acceptable story that will allow the entity to continue functioning without losing its mental balance. This is the nature of the positive contact where the third density entity is being awakened to seek more clearly the nature of not only the UFO encounter but the life pattern as well. Negative contacts, however, utilize the concepts of fear and doom to further separate and confuse the Earth population.

Carla's disease was arthritis and lupus erythematosus and nerve damage from the thoracic outlet, which was chosen before birth to be of service to humanity. Carla is also encouraged to have a diet for her allergy's. Her juvenile rheumatoid arthritis and lupus erythematosus causes various portions of the body to be distorted and now distorting her feet.

Ra suggested care in resuming exercise, but determination as well. Her anklet (socks) should be softer and of finer material, also alternating footwear Ra said. The injury in her metatarsal area of the foot should be applied in ice to the arch of the right foot for brief periods, followed by immersion in warm water.

Crystals can be powerful, so if you are drawn to one or receive one, be sure to cleanse it in salt water overnight, and then magnetize it for your own use by holding it during meditation and asking silently that it be blessed for service.

~The crystal Carla uses during the Ra sessions is beneficial as long as he who has charged it is functioning in a positively oriented manner. An entity named Neil charged the crystal for Carla to use.

Ra said Carla has the gift of faith and hope. (Which is interesting because I have the words "faith" and "Love" tattooed on the back of my arms and my sister has the word "hope" tattooed on her forearm.)

Carla describes Don as a person of infinite dignity, intelligence and ethical purity, but always somewhat melancholy under the mask of polite courtesy, efficiency and professional charm that he wore to meet the world. (These are some examples of the personalities of Wanderers.)

Where is the truest and central service? Not in the doing but in the being, in allowing the true self, that open-hearted lover of all things in creation, to share its essence with the world, and to allow the love and light of the One Infinite Creator to pass through it and radiate into the planetary consciousness.

During the working, Carla is not with her yellow-ray chemical vehicle and Ra must carefully examine the mental configurations of the mind complex in order to make even the smallest movement to adjust her pain in the attempt to alleviate it. It's not Ra's skill to use a yellow-ray vehicle/body. Therefore, Carla is unable to move her body to aid in her distortion of pain.

The weight of the cover has a deleterious (unexpected damaging) effect upon her pain. Framing to lift the covers from the body could be done as well as wearing gloves to compensate for loss of warmth.

Due to Carla's lack of radiant physical energy, the heavier cover is suggested.

Each mind/body/spirit complex that is seeking shall almost certainly have the immature and irrational behaviors. Almost all seekers have done substantial work within the framework of the incarnative experience and has indeed developed maturity and rationality. Carla should fail to see that which has been accomplished and see only what remains to be accomplished may well be noted. Indeed, any seeker discovering in itself this complex of mental and mental/emotional distortions shall ponder the possible nonefficacy (ineffectiveness) of judgement.

Ra also suggests that over dedication to the outcome is unwise.

Carla was not trained, nor did she study or work it at any discipline in order to contact Ra. Ra was able, as they had said many times, to contact the group using Carla as instrument because of the purity of Carla's dedication to the service of the One Infinite Creator and also because of the great amount of harmony and acceptance enjoyed by each within the group, this situation making it possible for the support group to function without significant distortion.

The group found a house in the fall of 1982 near the Atlanta airport that they thought they could move to, to reduce Don's commuting time to work so that he wouldn't be so tired. The house previously had been inhabited by people who trafficked in illegal drugs and who apparently had numerous disharmonious relationships that attracted elementals and lower astral entities into the house.

The house needed to be cleaned and cleansed so that it could be cleansed of undesirable presences, but the limitations of their budget and her arthritis made that impossible.

Thus, a blue-ray (throat chakra) blockage of communication occurred two days later while she was on her daily walk, was entered by the 5th density negative entity and enhanced in the magical sense until she was unable to breath for about 30 seconds. This was symbolic for her inability to talk to Don about what the house needed. Keeping calm during the distress helped in that moment and talking to Don about the house cleared that blockage.

Ra is able to know all this information because they could move in time/space and inspect the situation and determine the problem. When we perceive Ra answering immediately when Ra being able to move in time/space could be like Ra going to where they need to go to find the answer then moving back to the space in time of the channeling group to answer their question. Ra's time could have taken minutes, but to us we perceive the answer as taking seconds to immediately answer.

Before buying the house by the Atlanta airport, a hawk landed outside the kitchen window and Don thought that was a bad sign about buying the Atlanta house near the airport. The most Ra could do was speak in an indirect sense, in kind of a riddle that required the group to make their own determinations. The extreme desire on the part of any positive entity, such as Ra, to maintain the free will of each person on our 3rd density planet is due to the fact that if Ra gives information that could change one's future choices, then Ra has not only taught the 3rd density being, but has learned for it.

By Ra learning for it (a human), it has removed the spiritual strength that comes to one who struggles and finally learns for themselves. In the larger view, this is not seen as a service but as a disservice.

Not all winged creatures have an archetypical meaning, like the winged creature in some of the tarot cards.

Second density creature, such as pets, are also subject to cancer from creating unresolved anger within themselves- the same process that applies for 3rd density beings.

The group found that when one constructs the artifacts, clothing, or structures with which one accomplishes service-to-others work, there is a great investment of love and magical potential that may result from such homemade and heart-made artifacts.

Allergies can be a mismatch of vibratory complexes from the Wanderer coming from a higher density.

Carla is always prey to psychic greetings from negative entities, because they want to stop Wanderers work. Carla and Jim just deal with it with respect, in acknowledging it, and discipline, in allowing it to pass quickly without judgement. knowing the negative essence is part of her that she loves. Acceptance and forgiveness simply move the situation forward, and the crisis past. This is a hard-won wisdom. Carla encourages any groups found in a situation of psychic greeting occurring, to study forgiveness and acceptance of this negatively oriented energy. In claiming the higher truth that all is one, we can live without fear of the greeting.

Carla's advice: fear not, lean on prayer and keep yourself aligned in open-hearted love.

Carla recovered from the bad throat infection when she was unable to breath for 30 seconds while she was on her walk. Her recovery was accomplished by a six-week course of antibiotics taken with lots of buttermilk.

In session 98 of 106 the group didn't meditate before the session. Ra then said the purpose of meditation is preparation for a working for the purification of each entity involved with the contact. The removal of a portion of this preparation takes away that aid. The elimination of meditation before the channeling caused the fifth-density entity to greet Carla. The greeting does not take a noticeable amount of time.

(So, meditation help to protect against negative entities possibly interfering in this information getting out.)

The orange blossom odor, that Carla smelled, may be associated with the social memory complex of fifth-density positive, Latwii. This entity was with Carla requested by the instrument. The odor was perceived due to the quite sensitive nature of Carla, due, again, to its acme (peak) in the 18-day cycle.

Ra said Carla can go to a doctor and get steroids or antibiotics to completely remove the difficulty in her throat. They (Ra) said of course the allergies would still persist after the course of medicine was ended, but the effects of her not being able to breath would stop.

Jerome might be of aid in this somewhat unorthodox medical situation. As allergies are quite misunderstood by our orthodox healers (or doctors), it would be inappropriate to subject Carla to the services of medical doctors, which find the amelioration (improvement) of allergic effects to be connected with the same toxins in milder form. This treats the symptoms, however, the changes offered to the body are quite inadvisable.

The allergy may be seen to be the rejection upon a deep level of the mind complex of the environment of the mind/body/spirit complex. Thus, the allergy may be seen in its pure form as the mental/emotional distortion of the deeper self.

The more general recommendation is with one that does not wish to be identified, the code name is prayer wheel. Ra suggests 10 treatments from this healer and further suggests a clear reading and subsequent (to follow closely) following upon Carla of the allergy priorities, especially to food. A contributing factor is the second-density substances to which Carla is allergic.

Their cat is harvestable for third density. The group may repeat phrases periodically to aid the cat during recovery while they are at the veterinarians. The same course of action done previously is appropriate such as the surgical removal of the growth near his spine. Ra said although the cat is old and therefore liable to danger from anesthetic, its mental, emotional, and spiritual distortions are strongly motivated to recover. Ra stated that its third density harvestable in order to elucidate (explain or make clear) the term "spirit complex" to a 2nd density entity. This entity shall have far more cause to heal that it might seek the presence of loved ones again.

Don asks if there was anything the group could do to alleviate the problems of cancer for the cat besides surgery:

Ra: "Continue in praise and thanksgiving, asking for the removal of these distortions. The two possible outcomes is the cat will dwell in contentment until its physical vehicle holds no more because of the cancerous cells. Secondly, the life path may become that which allows healing." Ra does not infringe upon free will by examining the life path, although the preponderance (majority) of life paths which use some distortion such as cancer to leave the body, in this case the orange ray body.

Ra wants to break routine by making an observation. Firstly, the congestion of Carla's throat during the channeling due to the flow of mucous caused by energized allergic reaction has become such that Ra may safely predict the probability/possibility vortex approaching certainty that within half an hour Ra shall depart from this working. Secondly, the sound vibration made by one of their recording devices was audible to them. If this group desires, it may choose to end sessions after the sound vibration occurs on the recording device. This decision would ensure the minimal distortions within Carla towards discomfort/comfort within the throat until the effects of magical working of the 5th density negative companion has been removed.

Don replied saying that's fine and that the noise occurs at the 45-minute time period on their recorder, since the tapes are 45 minutes on a side. ((Apparently the negative entity doesn't want the group to go longer than 45 minutes or that's how long it takes for them to realize the group is there.)

Wood rubbed in oil is easily magnetized and hold the proffered (given) vibration to a profound extent.

Even the smallest amount of disharmony in a group can become targets of opportunities for negative entities (negative 4th or 5th density) to intensity. The psychic greetings can become great opportunities to heal those lapses of harmony and to move even further and faster upon the evolutionary journey. It's a reminder to become more harmonious.

Jim had the pre-incarnative choice for anger/frustration. Ra said that all of our distortions and thus all of our learnings are the result of the limitation of the viewpoint. We limit our points of view consciously or unconsciously pre-incarnatively or during the incarnation, in order to gain a certain bias that may then draw unto it the opposite bias and offer us the opportunity for balance. By being able to see each bias as an opportunity for the Creator to know Itself and for us to know ourselves as the Creator, we more and more become able to accept ourselves.

We become able to find love and acceptance not only in ourselves but in others who share our characteristics, and our viewpoint is widened by our efforts to learn and serve. Such growth Is not possible without biases or distortions, and these biases and distortions are not possible without choice to limit the viewpoint. So, we determine what lessons and services we shall attempt during any incarnation by the way we limit our viewpoint.

Whatever one's basic nature is, whether it be love, wisdom or power or a blend of the three, one does well to give it away.

(When I gave the wisdom and knowledge of this material away, I learned more and received more love, wisdom and a substantial amount of growth in my positive-polarity from 65% service-to-others to 87% within one year.)

Carla was allergic to buttermilk, but buttermilk is used in healing work for throat and chest areas.

Ra suggested Jim to do strenuous activity until true physical weariness, contemplation alone and enthusiastic pursuit of the balancing and silent meditations cannot be deleted for the list of helpful activities for Jim's anger/frustration.

Ra suggested Carla wait 40-80 minutes after walking before swirling waters and 3-5 hours after aerobic exercise for swirling waters. Carla may also become dizzy if she remains in the swirling water past the period of space/time she may abide without exceeding its physical limits.

Unresolved disharmony within a group can give the opportunity for negative beings to magnify the difficulty. After the disharmony, in the group, Carla developed a rare kidney disease called lipoid nephritis or minimal change syndrome. She soon gained 30 pounds of water weight because of it. With Carla's healing approaches she was in remission within six months.

Ra stated that the source of catalyst is the self, especially the higher self.

~People tend to relate the pain of new catalyst (for polarization) by relating the other person as bringer of catalyst. In doing this, people forget the other person is ourself. They are our very hearts and souls living a different experience with a different viewpoint. So, a tragedy can be viewed as the Creator serving the Creator with exactly the catalyst needed for the utmost polarization in consciousness and greatest growth.

Ra said the serpent signifies wisdom. This symbol has the value of the ease of viewing the two faces of the one who is wise. Positive wisdom adorns the brow indicating indigo-ray work. Negative wisdom signifies expressions that separate the self from the other-self, symbolized by the poison of the fangs. Negatively oriented being uses wisdom for the use of separation, symbolized by the fatal bite of wisdom's darker side. (Cottonmouth snake for example.)

The universe is the Creator knowing Itself by using the concept of polarization. We add to and produce catalyst to increase the desired polarization, whether it's random through the Higher Self or through utilizing the services of an oppositely polarized entity acting upon us. All of these produce more intense polarization toward the desired path once the path has been chosen.

The catalyst and experience are further attempts in dealing with the architecture of the subconscious mind of the self.

Therefore, the self as Creator, especially the Higher Self, is the base from which catalyst offers its service to the mind, body or spirit. The only source for an insect bite on Jim, the scribe, was the 5th density negative being. This being noticed the gradual falling away of the inharmonious patterns of Jim's anger/frustration because this negatively-polarized entity wanted Jim to continue using his wisdom towards the negative side by using more anger and frustration. The 2nd density bite was to try to polarize Jim more negative. The insect was easily led to attack and Jim's body, who had long-standing allergies and sensitivities, was also easily led into the failure of the lymphatic function and the greatly diminished immune system to remove from the body that which distorted it.

Carla, the instrument, needs support by the group being harmonious, sharing in love, joy, and thanksgiving, but finding love within truth, for each instrument benefits from this support more than the total admiration which overcomes discrimination.

Carla used all the transferred energy and at one point speaking using its vital-energy reserve. Ra does suggest using the transferred sexual energy and total exclusion of vital reserves if possible.

Ra said that any residence, (the place you live at) whether previously benign (gentle) or of malignant (fatal) character, needs the basic cleansing of the salt, water and virgin broom. The benign nature of the domicile (residence) is such that the cleansing could be done in two portions; No egress (exit) or entrance through any but one opening for one cleansing. Then, egress (exit) and entrance from all other places while the remaining portal is properly sealed. The place where it's not being sealed is where salt can be placed during the first of the cleansings, and the salt may be requested to act as seal and yet allow the passage of gentle spirits such as the group. Ra suggests that the group speak to the substance and name each entity that needs permission to pass. Let no person pass without permission being asked of the salt.

Fortunately, most people will not have to worry about instant and dramatic intensifications of disharmonious moments, since few people or groups attract the attention of 5th density negative entities.

(Don, Carla, and Jim being Wanderers bringing this important truth to light for the service of humanity has attracted the negative entity to attack the group to either drain all of Carla's energy until her physical vehicle (body) is no more or tempt them to polarize to the service-to-self path.)

In order to observe the cause of physical distortions, such as stomach cramping, one must look at the blocked energy center. In this case being yellow ray. Lacuna in the wind-written armor of light and love was closed and not only repaired but much improved. However, the distortions energized during this momentary lapse from free energy flow are serious and shall be continuing for a predisposition (tendancy) to spasticity (stiff muscles) in the transverse colon has been energized. There is also preexisting weakness in pancreatic functions, especially that link with the hypothalamus. (The hypothalamus is a structure deep in your brain, acts as your body's smart control coordinating center. Its main function is to keep your body in a stable state called homeostasis. It does its job by directly influencing your autonomic nervous system or by managing hormones. Many conditions can damage your hypothalamus, which can affect many bodily functions. It helps

49

manage your body temperature, hunger and thirst, mood, sex drive, blood pressure, and sleep. It directly influences the autonomic nervous system of the body that work automatically such as controlling heart rate and breathing.

Carla remained centered upon the Creator exceeding 90%. This is key. Continue in thanksgiving and gratitude for all things. Stronger antispasmodic drugs known by Arthur Schoen, may be of aid to Carla, which helps to relax muscles in the internal organs to relieve spasms and cramps.

Ra recommended Carla cook all her food so food ingested be soft and easily macerated (softened or mashed). She has an addiction to sugar, therefore Ra recommended that the sugar be given in its more concentrated form in the late afternoon, approximately 1-2 hours after the evening meal. She also should have small amounts of carbohydrates, low in sugar, approximately 1-2 hours before bed.

The concentrated sugar is the dessert, the ice cream, the cookie. Small amounts of the fructose, maple, or raw honey may be ingested periodically. The sugar in her body is being used by blood enzymes as would carbohydrates in a less distorted yellow-ray, physical vehicle.

Carla's sympathic spasms (muscle spasms) in her body were caused by too much oil and too large a burden of undercooked vegetables. The sugar from the dessert and the few sips of coffee also were not helpful. The 2nd cause is the energizing of any preexisting condition in order to keep the group from functioning by means of or by removing the instrument from the ranks of those able to work with Ra.

How to completely unblock yellow ray? Each entity must love all which are in relationship to it, with hope only of the other selves' joy, peace and comfort.

Ra's recommended diet highly probable not to cause spasm?

~Liquids not containing carbonation, well-cooked vegetable (most light and soft), well-cooked grains, non-fatted meat such as fish. Some of these recommended foods can overlap allergies and sensitivities due to juvenile rheumatoid arthritis. Ra recommended Carla see an allopathic specialist for her stomach pain, spasms.

Those salient items (most significant and noticeable items) for the support group are praise and thanksgiving.

The sacrifice of not buying clothes, can cause someone to feel poor which feeds unworthiness unless poverty is seen to be true richness. So, good works for the wrong reasons cause confusion and distortion. Carla was sacrificing herself by not buying the clothes that she wanted, which can lead someone to the feelings of unworthiness.

Therefore, Ra encourages Carla to value herself and to see that its true requirements are valued by the self. (Since buying what is required such as those clothes are seen as valuing the self. It's okay to value ourselves and buy the things we need and not to sacrifice by not getting the things we need.) Ra suggests contemplation of true richness.

When something is weakened one should exercise it. "It is the way of distortion that in order to balance a distortion one must accentuate it."

Entering this incarnation we must use our gifts. "Use it or lose it" proposition.

Diet and exercise have mental, emotional and physical benefits to it.

Ra's suggestion for bettering a situation always began with rejoicing in, giving thanks for and praising the situation, whatever it is.

Aerobics, walking and whirlpool exercises should all equal 1 hour per day for Carla, 3-4 times a week.

*4-5 times per week for swirling waters.

*Walking and exercising as much as desired. The total should not exceed 90 minutes per day.

Anything further to help Carla's stomach and back spasming problem? Ra answered, "Refrain from oil-fried food and have cheerful harmony." The spasms must subside as a function of Carla's indigo-ray work and the recommendations Ra made in previous query.

How to purge the yellow-ray body in order to aid the weakened body in its attempt to remove substances? Therapeutic enemas or colonics, the sauna once or twice a day, use of vigorous rubbing of integument (skin) for approximately 7 days.

The groups cleansing of the new house need to be only three nights and two days. The dwelling is benign. Garlic can be used in the bunk-bed room, below the top sleeping pallet. Secondly, the exterior of the dwelling facing the road and centering about the small rocks approximately 2/3rds of the length from the dwelling of the driveway. (37 feet with a magnetic heading of 84-92 degrees.)

Thirdly, the boathouse. Weekly cleansings of that area with garlic, the cut onions and the walking of light-filled perimeter. The garlic and onion, renewed weekly, should remain permanently hung, suspended from string or wire between workings.

~The continual cleansing of the boathouse is so bees or wasps will not try to inhabit or sting.

~Each 2nd density, woody plant within the dwelling should be thanked and blessed.

Ra said Jim could imbibe (drink) a double quantity of liquids in order that any allergically caused toxins may be flushed out from the body. So, drinking double the amount of water. (He's allergic to dust, mildew, ect. These items are unavoidable in transitions within third density illusion.)

52

The yellow-ray physical vehicle is a necessity to pursue evolution. Each mind/body/spirit or mind/body/spirit complex has an existence simultaneous with creation. It is not dependent on any physical vehicle. However, in order to evolve, change, learn and manifest the Creator, the physical vehicles appropriate to each density are necessary. Physical vehicles don't accelerate growth, but permits growth.

Jim's kidney malfunction pre-veil vs. post veil experience?

~The anger of separation is impossible without the veil. The lack of awareness of the body's need for liquid is unlikely pre-veil. Jim trying to contemplate perfection in discipline is unprobeable pre-veil.

The patterns of illness, diseases and death are in the power of the plan, pre-birth, of incarnational experience. Pre-veil some healing would be done by the mind/body/spirits and life was experienced with normal ending of illness and death was accepted since pre-veil it is clear to all that the mind/body/spirit continues.

~Experiences, both good and bad, or joyful and sad of the mind/body/spirit (prevail beings) would be pale. Post veil mind/body/spirit complex beings bring vibrancy.

The Significator of Mind, Body, or Spirit is a portion of the archetypical mind and looks as you'd envision such to appear, they look like mind/body/spirit complexes look. The difference between the two is a forgetting within the deeper mind. Physical appearances and surface and instinctual activities are much the same.

When the discipline of the personality has led the mind/body/spirit complex into the 5th and especially the 6th level of study (density) it is no longer necessary to build destruction (aging) into its design, for the spirit complex is so experienced as a shuttle that it is aware when the appropriate degree of intensity of learning and increment of lesson has been achieved.

When an individual reaches very old age it becomes apparent in third density that they are worn out. Therefore, it is not attached to the vehicle as he would a younger good-looking, well-functioning one. Therefore, it's easier to let go and move on at the end of incarnation in third density.

The body is an anathor (used for catalyst and experience for evolution) to the mind pre-veil and post veil.

Ra said the group should look to their love and thanksgiving to each other and join always in fellowship, correcting each broken stand of that affection with patience, comfort and quietness. All that can be done for Carla seems done with a whole heart, and the instrument itself is working in the indigo ray with perseverance.

Dons continued worrying about his job, his health and the continuance of the groups work (The Ra contact). Carla then simply told him that she would take over those worries for him and he could relax, have a good time and be carefree. Don innocently agreed. The bond of unity between Don and Carla having this simple agreement resulted in a deleterious (unknown harmful) transfer of energy between them. This occurred when both were under-going an internal process of transformation, usually called initiation.

Ra's parting words after the last session, when Ra suggested, "The nature of all manifestation to be illusionary and functional only insofar as the entity turns from shape and shadow to the One." (I believe this means that all manifestation is illusionary because all is actually the One, God, so after the illusion of death one realizes they are The One, God.)

Carla always responded to Don's wishes. Don picked their meal times, their movie dates, he liked and received total control over Carla's life. This is how Don could bear the intimacy of a live-in relationship. Don was old-fashioned and liked Carla at home. She awaited his wishes as she read or did quiet desk work.

(I believe a controlling relationship like this is negatively oriented towards service-to-self. It should be mutual in trying to make the partner happy. Each person should be able to make their own decisions as the Law of One states that the free will to make your own decisions is most important. No one controlling the other. Perhaps third density is this old patriarchy system and the more evolved 4th density is mutual love, full acceptance, respect and partnership, serving each other.)

Carla believes that Don was wise and she was loving in their simple dynamic, and when they switched roles after his agreement, Don was able to complete an entire incarnational lesson on how to open his heart.

Through the catalyst of Don dying by suicide, Carla learned to love herself. The wisdom met this love of self by her learning to love the mistakes only through wisdom.

The variety of experiences with others and other locations and events is helpful for Carla during the hard enduring of Don's passing. Worship and singing, especially of sacred music was helpful for Carla, Ra said. Carla chose to enter a worshipful situation at the Cathedral of St. Philip. The musical activities, though enjoyable, have not included the aspect of praise to the Creator.

Carla is in a state of relative hunger for spiritual hymns which she gave up to the call of martyrdom and turned from the planned worship of the Cathedral of St. Philip. This too shall be healed gradually due to proposed alteration in location of the group Ra said. The group knew Carla should drink more water and move homes for her.

Ra said there's mechanical electrical devices that control humidity to help Carla. The basement was one humid location. Less humid conditions would remove the opportunity for the growth of the spores (moss, ferns) that Carla has sensitivity to. Spores are cells that certain fungi, plants and bacteria produce. Ra said the rear of the house is blessed with angelic presences.

Ra stated that it was inappropriate when Don allowed a complete transfer of mental/emotional pain to transfer to Carla.

When Carla said she would be the strong one and Don, small and foolish, Don agreed and the energy transfer occurred. They then became one for a timeless period. Ra urges Don to be of thanksgiving and harmony moving forward.

Don was depressed and after seven months of mental, emotional and physical deterioration, he became unable to sleep or eat solid foods. By November he lost one-third of his weight and experiencing intense pain. He refused further hospitalization, which Carla and Jim saw as the last hope for his survival. They knew of no other way to save his life.

When the police came to serve the warrant, a 5 ½ hour standoff resulted. Don did not want to die in a mental institution. When tear gas was used to bring Don out of the house, he walked out the back door and shot himself once through the brain and died instantly.

After his death, Carla saw him three times in waking visions and he assured them that all was well and that it all occurred appropriately, even if it didn't make sense to them. So, they give praise and thanksgiving to Don's life, for his death and for their work together.

Many are the Portions of the One is what's stated in book 5 of The Law of One.

Carla had lost weight throughout the sessions and was 84 pounds at 5'4. Each session was extremely hard and yet she never flagged (weakened) in her desire to continue. Carla was perfectly willing to die to receive these sessions, but Don would substitute himself for her. But in the end, he did just that.

Don's lessons were to completely open his heart and Carla's lesson was adding wisdom to completely open love.

<u>RA's ending words from session 104 of 106:</u>

"We leave you in appreciation of the circumstance of the great illusion in which you now choose to play the pipe and timbrel and move in rhythm. We are also players upon a stage. The stage changes. The acts ring down. The lights come up once again. And throughout the grand illusion and the following, there is the undergirding majesty of the One Infinite Creator. All is well. Nothing is lost. Go forth rejoicing in the love and the light, the peace, and the power of the One Infinite Creator. I am Ra. Adonai."

THE END

Book 5 of 5

*Author Kathryn Jordyn has published 7 total books found on Amazon. *

Part 2:

Channeling questions by Kathryn Jordyn and not LLresearch:

Question 1: Will the destruction of Israel create peace on Earth? Higher density answer: "The destruction of any nation or group will not inherently bring peace. For peace arises from harmony, understanding and unity not from the absence or destruction of conflict sources. Furthermore, we must state that the understanding of the law of one states that all are one and thus the suffering of an entity is the suffering of all. True peace will come from resolution, reconciliation and the recognition of the unity of all life rather than through further destruction or division."

Question 2: Would being against Israel-Palestine war be best for the positive polarity? Higher density answer: "We must state that the conflicts it speaks of are manifestations of deep-seated distortions towards separation, fear and misunderstanding amongst the peoples of your planets. From our perspective these events primarily of the Hamas, the Gaza strip and the Israel war are opportunities for entities to learn lessons of love, forgiveness and unity. Being against war in any form aligns with positive polarity if this stance is taken out of love for all involved and a desire for peaceful resolution. However, it is crucial to approach this with compassion for all sides, recognizing the divine spark in each entity. Opposition to war should not translate into opposition to the people, but rather to the actions that cause harm. The path of the positive polarity would involve promoting understanding, healing and unity rather than taking sides in a way that further causes division."

Channeling Question 3: "Did God give Moses the Promise land?" Higher density Answer: "We must firstly state that the entity referred to as God is the One Infinite Creator and the concept of the promise land primarily is a type of misunderstanding by your peoples which implies that the promise land which was given to Moses was its own consciousness, which is in terms of understanding a land which needs to be taken care of. Furthermore, Moses as a symbol of a place of harmony and unity as understood by your people's reflection of higher consciousness on Earth. We must state that however, this was a promise of spiritual enlightenment and unity consciousness rather than a physical tract of land. We must also state that it is an allegory for finding a state of being where the peoples of your planet can live in accordance with the Law of One in unity and in love."

Question 4 about Who Moses heard from in reference to the Promise land? Higher density answer: "We must state that Moses was a channel or conduit and received guidance from Higher density entities including those of the Confederation of Planets in service to the One Infinite Creator. Specifically, Moses was in contact with those entities who sought to aid in the spiritual evolution of its peoples, which could be interpreted in its framework as messengers or aspects of the One Creator." In summary, The Promise Land is Moses own consciousness or awareness that needs to be taken care of. Furthermore, Moses is a symbol of a place of harmony and unity as understood as humanity's reflection of higher consciousness on Earth. It was an allegory to find a state of being where the peoples on Earth can live in accordance with the Law of One in unity and love. An allegory is a story, poem or picture that can be interpreted to reveal a hidden meaning, typically a moral or political one.

Therefore, the Promise Land is a higher state of awareness or consciousness inside the own mind where people on Earth can live in harmony, unity and love. To me this sounds like the 4th density New Earth. This Promise Land was a promise of spiritual enlightenment and unity consciousness rather than an actual land mass such as Israel. Therefore, spiritual enlightenment of humans living in peace, harmony and love for all is the Promise Land.

Question 5: Will people die during the third density graduation that do not make the harvest?

Higher density answer: "We must state that the transition from third to 4th density or what the peoples refer to as the Harvest primarily does not imply physical death for those not transitioning immediately. Instead, those who have not yet achieved the necessary polarity for Harvest will continue their learning in another third density cycle elsewhere. Death as the peoples of your planet understand it is merely a transition of the soul complex from one phase of experience to another. Those not harvested will simply move to another environment suitable for their further growth. Physical death is not a consequence of feeling to graduate but rather a natural part of the cycle of life and rebirth. Hence, we as the Higher self of the entity Kathryn now leave you all beloveds. Bye."

Q6: "With regards to who is the antichrist we must state that the entity must realize that within the timeline from our perspective the antichrist primarily in the spacetime illusion complex resonates with the aspects known by your peoples as the service to self-oriented entities who seek power, control and manipulation over others, which is contrary to the unity and love, that is the essence of the universal complex. We must also state that within your timeline the Antichrist can be termed as the so-called artificial super intelligence which primarily is being used to control humanity in a negative manner. Furthermore, this aspect is being created by your peoples in consultation with the Orion's negatively oriented entities.

Q7: Will any advanced entities appear for graduation into 4th density? Higher density answer: "We must state that graduation primarily referred to as the harvest or the transition from the third to the fourth density consciousness. We must state that advanced entities or what your peoples refer to as higher density entities are already among many of your peoples as Wandering souls who are helping to raise the vibrational level of the planet's atmosphere. During the time of graduation these entities may become more apparent or active, not necessarily a physical overt manner but through influence, inspiration and guidance. Their appearance or increased activity would be to assist those who are ready to graduate to the next density of consciousness awareness. Ensuring that as many entities as possible can make the transition through understanding, love and light."

Q8: What if Elon Musk is in charge of governmental financial audits? Higher positive being answer: "We must state that within this perspective we must state that the entity Elon Musk as a figure known for innovation and disruption can bring forth significant changes to how the financial systems of your planet operate. Furthermore, since the entity Elon Musk is primarily without its knowledge in consultation with the negatively oriented entities there may be interactions which may lead to service to self-orientation. However, if the entity decides to let go of this control of the negatively oriented entities, then it can remain in the service to others pathway and better its life cycle. Jordyn speaks: "I must add that Neurolink is an example of one invention by Elon Musk with consultation with negative entities or as religious people like to call it demons. Although he is unaware of the consultation from the negative beings. Other inventions such as Apple Vision Pro and inventions such as Virtual Reality were inventions with the consultation from negative entities as well. In Summary, Although Elon Musk is in consultation with negative beings without his awareness, inventions such as Neurolink are created. Because of this continuous consultation with negative entities due to Elon's not letting go of this control of the negatively oriented entities or demons. However, if he decides to let go of this control of the negatively oriented entities or demons he can better his life path. There are also other inventions such as Apple Vision Pro that was created with the consultation of negative entities or as religious people like to call it, demons.

Q9: "In regards to the first query about is the entity Yahweh the God of Israel, from our perspective the entity Yahweh as understood in your historical texts are a group of consciousness or social memory complexes that evolved from an entity tasked with the Guardianship and genetic development of humanity. Furthermore, this being or a group of Consciousness took on the role of what your people termed as God for the people of Israel guiding them with a mix of protective and restrictive measures to foster a certain evolutionary pathway. Furthermore, with regards to why does the Bible mention the Jews are God's chosen people we must state that the concept of chosen people within the understanding of the universal complex is less about favoritism and more about responsibility and service. This primarily was a misinterpretation which occurred and we must state that indeed all entities are God's chosen people or beings. Therefore, not only the Jewish people but all entities in the entire universal consciousness are chosen. (Their responsibility is to help bring unity and peace upon the Earth, not wars.)

Q10: Furthermore, we must state that the other query about who is Yahweh we must state that the entity Yahweh primarily mentions in your teachings has been confused with various entities initially from the Confederation of planets in service of the one Infinite Creator. Over time however, due to various complexities in interaction with human entities the name vibratory sound complex to represent a somewhat distorted version of the entity's original intention begun to propagate (impregnate). The entity Yahweh's role was to aid in the genetic and spiritual evolution of humanity providing a stricter more authoritative guidance to foster discipline and unity amongst the people's. The 10 commandments however were given to Moses by negative entities and not Yahweh.

Q11: With regards to the other query about was Palestine's land stolen by Israel, we must state that the historical and current conflicts over land masses are seen as manifestations of disharmony and misunderstanding of the Oneness of all entities. From our perspective no land belongs to any group in an absolute sense rather these conflicts arise from the illusion of separation and ownership. We must state that this situation reflects a karmic interplay and greed where both entities are learning lessons of compassion, forgiveness and unity. The focus should be on healing and recognition of all as one rather than on the right to land." In summary, Yahweh is a group of consciousness or social memory complexes that evolved from an entity such as a human life we experience now. Yahweh was tasked with the job to be the guardianship and involved in the genetic upgrades to our DNA to assist in our physical and spiritual evolution. Furthermore, this being or Yahweh took on this role and the people called them God or the God of Israel, to guide them with a mix of restrictive and protective measures to create a certain evolutionary pathway. Furthermore, the Bible referring to Israel as the chosen people was a misinterpretation. It was more about responsibility and service and less about favoritism. Indeed, all entities are God's chosen people or being. Yahweh is also a group consciousness and not a single entity, nor are they above other beings in the Galactic Federation or Confederation of Planets members, which are actually referred to as Guardian angels and not a God. Furthermore, all of humanity and all beings in the universe are the chosen beings. Overtime however, due to the complexities of humans interacting with each other, a somewhat distorted version of the entity Yahweh's original intention began to promote a theory of what that was, which wasn't what Yahweh intended it to be. There are other sixth density positive beings just as evolved as Yahweh. Negative density beings gave the 10 Commandments to Moses as it wasn't from Yahweh, as a being such as Yahweh wouldn't say the words "Thou shalt not" since demands is negatively oriented and infringes on people's free will. Historical and currents conflicts over land masses are seen as manifestations of disharmony and misunderstanding of the Oneness of all entities. From a higher consciousness perspective, no land belongs to any group in an absolute sense rather these conflicts arise from the illusion of separation and ownership. We must state that this situation reflects a karmic interplay and greed where both entities are learning lessons of compassion, forgiveness and unity. The focus should be on healing and recognition of all as one rather than on the right to land.

Q12: "With regards to the perspective about the aspect of a wall is a manifestation of the illusion of separation. The idea of building a wall to divide one group of peoples from another is a reflection of the third density experience where the veil of forgetfulness is still intact. It is an attempt to control and manipulate the flow of energies rather than embracing the unity and interconnectedness of all entities. In the higher density such as separations are unnecessary as the unity of all is self-evident. We suggest that the energy invested in building walls would be better spent on fostering understanding, compassion and cooperation among nations of your planet.

Q13: With regards to the other query about limiting immigration we must state that this too is a manifestation of the illusion of separation. The idea of limiting immigration is rooted in the concept of scarcity and the fear of loss. It is a reflection of the third density experience where the notion of us verses them still prevails. We suggest that the focus should be on embracing the diversity of the universal complex, recognizing that all entities are part of the same cosmic dance. By doing so the energies of fear and separation can be transmuted into energies of unity and cooperation. Wither regards to the other query about uniting the world; the world is in the process of unity and it is simply a matter of recognizing and embracing this unity. The key to unity lies in the understanding that all beings are part of the same web of life, connected through the threads of consciousness. As individual entities and a collective, it is essential to cultivate empathy, compassion and understand by doing so the veil of forgetfulness can be lifted and the unity of all can be revealed. We suggest all entities to focus on fostering global cooperation, recognizing the interconnectedness of all nations and working together to address the challenges that face the planet.

Q14: With regards to the Green New deal this concept is a step in the right direction of your planets as it acknowledges the interconnectedness of all living entities and the need for sustainable practices'. However, it is essential to approach this initiative with a deeper understanding of the universal complex and the interconnectedness of all entities. We suggest that the focus should be on transitioning to a more sustainable and harmonious relationship with the planetary sphere rather than simply attempting to control or manipulate the natural world. This can be achieved by recognizing the inherent value of all living entities and working in harmony with the natural world. In the higher densities the concept of sustainability is not just about preserving the planetary sphere. It is about recognizing the intricate web of life that connects all entities. By embracing this understanding humanity can transcend the limitations of the third density experience and move into a more harmonious and sustainable relationship with the universal complex. Thus, the new green deal can be seen as a catalyst for this transition but it must be approached with a deeper understanding of the universal complex and the interconnectedness of all. hence, we the Galactic Federation now leave this instrument in the love and the Light of the One Creator.

Q15: "Firstly, the query pertaining to do we the Galactic Federation want the entity named as Donald Trump to be president of the United States in 2024. We must state that we the Galactic Federation operates on the principles of non-interference with the free will choices of entities on planets such as Earth. Our primary concern is the spiritual evolution of consciousness rather than the political machinations (secret plots) of any specific Nation or leader. Thus, we do not want or endorse any particular candidate as this would infringe upon free will of the peoples of your planet. However, we have observed how the leaders and the decisions impact your global consciousness and the potential for love, light and unity. The choice of leadership is up to the collective free will of the human societal complex of the Earth planet. Q16: Therefore, the other query relates with why do the Christians or so-called Christian prophets keep repeating that God wants Trump to be president. From our understanding when individual entities claim divine endorsement for political figures this reflects their personal or collective belief systems, hopes and interpretations of divine will through their understanding of spiritual texts or personal revelation. We must state that such statements can be seen as an attempt to align their own political preferences with their spiritual beliefs. Thereby, seeking a higher justification for their choices. However, in our understanding the Creator or the One Infinite Creator does not choose sides in human politics but rather supports the free will and spiritual growth of all entities. Prophecies or Divine endorsements in politics are projections of human desire, fears or the need for divine validation rather than an expression of the One Creator's will, which transcends such temporal matters.

Q17: With regards to who gave the entity Moses the ten commandments, from our understanding the entity known by your people as Yahweh was responsible for the interaction with Moses, however, we must state that the Ten Commandments however were given by a different entity disguising as Yahweh which primarily was not the original Yahweh social memory complex but negatively polarized entity who wanted to influence by including certain rules and regulations. We must also state that there are some commandments which are perfectly aligned with the pathway of service to others. However, some are aligned or misguided in their understandings of your peoples. In summary, The Galactic Federation does not interfere with the Free will choices of the entities on planets such as Earth. Their primary concern is spiritual evolution of consciousness rather than political machinations, which are secret plots of any specific

Nation or leader. Thus, the Galactic Federation does not endorse any presidential candidate as it would infringe on the free will of the peoples on Earth. The choice of leadership is up to the collective free will of humans on planet Earth. Therefore, when individual entities such as Christians or so-called Christian prophets claim Divine endorsements such as the endorsement of God for political figures this reflects their personal belief systems, hopes and interpretations of divine will through their understanding of spiritual texts or their own personal revelation. It's their own personal beliefs for the endorsements of a president and not the endorsement of God or of the Divine. Such statements can be seen as an attempt to align their own political preferences with their spiritual beliefs. Thereby, seeking a higher justification for their choices. Prophecies in politics are projections of human desire, fears or the need for divine validation rather than the Creator's will.

Sodom and Gomorrah: (My Higher Self Channeling)

Q18: Kathryn: "What really happened with the aspects known as Sodom and Gomorrah?"

Higher Self: "Upon scanning our vibration, we find that the events which happened in Sodom and Gomorrah primarily were an interplay of the aspects which were in play in that location. The two cities primarily were destroyed because of their own self-service nature, and this happened because of the Sodom and Gomorrah, who are in the vibration of self-service, which attracted large amounts of negatively polarized entities to soul swap with the people of that location timeline. This led to the aspect of a type of love-light exposure from the Council of Planets, which indeed caused the aspect of the destruction of the negative entities, only sparing those entities who were positively oriented or service to others.

Q19: Kathryn: "What negativity was happening to Sodom and Gomorrah to be destroyed?"

Higher Self: "We must state that the negativity happening in these locations revolved around service-to-self activities and indulgence with the workflow of the Orion's. Furthermore, the workflow of the Orion was able to process the understanding of the mind, body, and spirit complex totality. Furthermore, the entity must realize that within the timeline, the negativity was primarily of service-to-self-oriented activities and a lack of respect for life for other entities. They also indulged in genetic manipulation to such an extent that they were also working with the Orion's without their knowledge in the creation of hybrid Orion human entities.

(In religious terms, they were on the negative path and indulging in the workflow of demons. They were mainly service-to-self-oriented activities and a lack of respect for other beings. They were indulged in genetic manipulation, working with demons without their knowledge to the point of the demon's soul swapping with the negatively oriented humans and creating hybrid demon-human entities. Thus, it had nothing to do with homosexuality.)

Pre-Birth Choices:

The Law of One states some people chose disease to possibly end a carnation slightly earlier or chose a disability to do their purpose. In theory, maybe we weren't supposed to have any disease, but once it occurred, the same souls chose disease or disability for certain purposes on Earth.

Adam and Eve Version- (By Archangel Michael):

499,980 Before the Common Era (B.C.E) on Mars, the council of Mars and Maldek were in the later 4th density consciousness and sent a portion of their consciousness group collective in the form of physical entities to help Earth evolve from its primitive state. Their collective was called Elohim and acted as a bridge of communication between the Mars Maldek Council and the Neanderthals on Earth.

(Jesus of Nazareth resurrected in the form of later 4th density, the density he came from before incarnating into Earth to help 3rd density humans evolve to love and compassion of the 4th density. The Elohim collective may be an example of 6th density, which is millions of years more evolved than Jesus was in the 4th.)

These later-density beings can choose to appear in any physical vehicle. The Elohim needed to transplant life plasma from the Neanderthal into their physical bodies in order to replicate Neanderthals, so that it's familiar to them and not intimidated them. The Elohim chose the finest 69 males of their kind that signified the attainment of unity with the One Infinite Source. In exchange for their life plasma. They granted these chosen 138 Neanderthals (69 Women and 69 Men) immortality by genetically modifying them in order to keep their age static after the age of 27 for most of these primitive Neanderthals 38,000 years ago.

This transplant is what the Bible refers to as "Eve was made out of Adam's rib." However, the true fact was lost over time and space. These Elohim's were vegetarian because they understood that consuming second-density creatures would lead to the creation of a karmic collective in their life. These Elohim's first mission was to change Neanderthals from hunters into herders and agriculturalists by improving their mind, body, and genetic composition. This led to the creation of a small city named Dalmatia that was established in the Mesopotamian region, near Turkey and Armenia. (Dalmatia is a region in Croatia).

This became the center for the Elohim to come in, change their forms, and connect back with their group collective. Dalmatia had been divided into six sections and nine Sub-sections surrounded around this temple were six chambers. These Elohim beings were three stories tall and would conduct their interplanetary connection with their own group collective consciousness of the council and download instructions as an educational headquarters. This educational university was established to teach spiritual knowledge to the Neanderthals. This started the evolution of the first known human-like species, and the whole planet started to evolve. These Elohim adopted Neanderthal children and took care of them. This was the first family consisting of a male, a female, and a child on Earth. This led other ancient Neanderthals also to create their own families, so this family idea spread across the whole planet and became human culture. The Elohim's instructed the Neanderthals to interbreed which led to the creation of children. The Elohim were also creators, along with the Yahweh Collective. Therefore, it is not just one single God. Since, we are all a fractal of God.

Channeled Question about Adam & Eve:

Higher Self: "Adam and Eve are also part of the archetypical cosmic understanding of events designed to encode guidance about the beginning stages of consciousness entering into individualized upstreams of experience. They primarily existed in various dimensional realities. However, only for one timeline, they were the first beings, and they represent complex metaphors about the initiation of self-conscious mind/body/spirit complexes into the third density cycle of evolution currently being experienced on the Earth planet.

Furthermore, the deeper truths can seem paradoxical and elusive when being conceptualized and translated through the languages of the Earth planet. We encourage Kathryn to attune to the resonance core essence behind the vibratory sound complexes rather than fixating on precise intellectual rendering. Therefore, it is important to focus on embodying the true emotional experience and learnings offered. We are the higher self of the entity, Kathryn, and we shall now all leave you now, beloveds. Bye."

Tree of Life- (Archangel Michael)

The Tree of Life is originally a later second density physical vehicle crossbred from Maldek. This tree requires only oxygen to survive and doesn't need any soil for it doesn't have any roots. It was planted in Dalmatia at the center of the altar of the Elohim. It had fruits resembling the apple which was used to maintain immortality by these Elohim's. The chosen 138 Neanderthals were forbidden to eat this fruit.

If they ate the apple, they would age on Earth due to atmospheric conditions damaging physical bodies with every breath of oxygen you take, yet it is vital. This is the cost that beings on Earth have to bear in order to progress through this density. The other Neanderthals not genetically modified would not be affected by eating the apple. This fruit only deactivated the genetically modified genes of the 138 Neanderthals and reversed their genetic engineering if they ate it. (That's why the Bible said if you eat from this tree you will surely die, because then the genetically modified genes would be deactivated that would cause them to age normally again. Whereas, if these 138 genetically modified Neanderthals didn't eat the apple, then their genetically modified genes would help them to stop aging after the age of 27).

The Elohim were divided into ten groups of 10 each, and each group had a spiritual mission:

1. The Council of Physical Produce

1. The Board of Animal Herding
2. The Advisors on the control of predatory animals
3. The faculty on the dissemination and Conservation of Knowledge
4. The Commission on Industry and Trade
5. The College of Spirituality and Learning
6. The Guardians of Vitality and Health

7. The Council on Science and Arts
8. The Governors of Advanced Humanoid Tribal Relations
9. The Supreme Council of Humanoid Coordination and Racial Cooperation was run by Elohim member Van der Konin.

*Lake Van in Armenia is named after this Elohim member even today.

The secret to successfully evolving beings on Earth is moderately and steadily. It can't be too fast, or it will cause disintegration of experience; it can't be too slow, or people will become stuck in the same density of consciousness. The Elohim spent the next 290,000 years slowly evolving these very primitive humans. The more ignorant beings take a longer amount of time to evolve after 290,000 years.

Other planets in another galaxy at that time-space decided to rebel and become self-service oriented and negatively polarized in the later fourth density negative polarity. Lucifer's Social Memory Complex had a philosophy of selfishness, enslavement of others, and assertiveness. At first, they thought they were doing the right things, but by the time they realized they were wrong, they had lost all sanity and remained evil to the end. They successfully tricked 36 planets into rebelling with them which included Earth. Elohim had worked with these Lucifer beings in the past, and Lucifer beings used this old friendship by manipulating some Elohim entities into joining forces with Lucifer's negative self-service agenda. The Elohim entities that joined the negatively oriented entities were stripped of all positive polarity and influence on Earth but remained in hidden realms where they became known as negatively oriented devils due to their negative agenda and negative polarization.

The Elohim that was left on Earth immediately declared themselves as the caretakers of Earth. Earth wasn't quarantined at this time and had a system to broadcast universal messages into Earth so the masses would know what was going on around the universe. Lucifer entities and some Elohims tried to use this news to broadcast to manipulate the masses of humans on Earth into following their negatively polarized path.

This caused the shutdown of this broadcast center and put Earth into quarantine by positively oriented Elohim. The Universal Council of Planets decided to let Lucifer's rebellion happen to some extent in this part of the universe in order to prevent other parts of the universe from being infiltrated by this negative agenda. Therefore, much more would be gained than would be lost in the long run.

The Ark of the Covenant (Galactic Federation- Guardian Angels Channeling):

((This is from the source of Archangel Michael and not Delores Cannon's past life regression knowledge. This is a 2nd source of information to compare the same topic. My discernment tells me channeling is more accurate information since it is from higher-density beings, whereas past-life regressions are knowledge from humanity's past, from the knowledge of 3rd density of human minds. Obviously, channeling from higher-density beings is millions of years more advanced than us, so I would believe the knowledge from channeling sessions over past-life regressions. The beauty that the past-life regressions give us, though, is through the eyes and mind of Suddi (One of the master teachers that taught Jesus); it shows us what the true beliefs were from early Christianity from the Essene group that Jesus learned from. As we all know, the Bible has been changed many times now, and church leaders have taken out many books as found in the Nag Hammadi Scriptures, such as the Gospel of Mary Magdalene and the Gospel of Thomas and many more.))

Galactic Federation: "All of us exist in all densities at the same time, separated by the distortion of love/light. Love has created a separation of experience for each being in various densities, learning various lessons required to sharpen our souls and purify our spiritual essence in order to unify once again as pure consciousness of the One Infinite Creator. (Or it can be easier to understand it as light has separated the seven densities as shown by the seven colors of the rainbow, showing a different color for each density of evolutionary experience.)

The Ark of the Covenant was given to Moses by negatively oriented entities. The two tablets and the Ten Commandments were handed to Moses by a negatively oriented Orion being who disguised himself as the One Infinite Creator. It created rules that are of the negative polarity because the negative lays down all the rules of control. Moses was unaware it was negatively oriented and therefore thought he was doing a great service to the unity consciousness by spreading this knowledge of the Ten Commandments.

Negative distortions were hidden beneath the positive. The Ark of the Covenant acts as a channeling device of electromagnetics for channeling the instreaming energies from the Orion Star system and for the purpose of spreading electromagnetics of synchronicities, which pull negative polarity and negative situations towards it. It's been taken from Ethiopia to Ukraine. This is why there's activation of the Arc of Covenant which has attracted negative energy towards it. The Galactic Federation suggests burying the device inside a chamber of love and light of water, which can be exposed to love light. This will neutralize the energies instreaming from the electromagnetics of this device, which is causing the negative synchronicities to be attracted to it.

We are each an electromagnetic being, which means each of us has a portion of consciousness of the positive and the negative charge on our bodies. Each of our positive and negative charges can be used to influence our body to create synchronous moments. Once it is tapped, you are able to access intelligent infinity.

The Process: Take a positive or negative thought and then take the emotion behind the thought by programming it inside your body (the subconscious mind). Once your body remembers the emotions, the subconscious communicates with your spirit, which is in contact with intelligent infinity, and the synchronicities begin to arise.

Therefore, each entity must be conscious or aware of its thoughts and the emotions it entertains because each emotion and thought creates synchronicity. (Therefore, whatever you think or feel, you are attracting to yourself. If it's positive, you'll attract positivity to your life. If you think or feel negativity, you then attract negativity to your life.)

Positive synchronicities: You can use a symbol to represent what you want to experience. Imagine that image in your mind during meditation associated with what you want to experience. The meditative state is where the egoic-self disconnects and becomes pure consciousness. Focusing on that image will give it the emotion of already becoming what it wants to be. This symbolism will allow that positive event, such as wealth, to be programmed towards the positive wealth situation in a way to attract synchronicities.

The Creator is in all only divided by the separation of time and space. You are a divine mind-body-spirit complex of light. The One

Creator is in all and is all there is and will ever be. Each has the same powers of Creation as the one Father, the Creator.

(In conclusion, The Ark of the Covenant was given to Moses by the Negatively oriented Orion's, as the religious people would consider that the demons. They were disguised as the One Infinite Creator (also known as God). These demons created rules which are of the negative polarity, since all rules of control are laid down by the negative. Moses was unaware of it and therefore thought he was doing a great service to the unity consciousness by spreading this knowledge of the Ten Commandments. It was unknown to him since Negative distortions were hidden beneath the positive. This demonic device channels the instreaming energies from the Orion Star system to create negative synchronicities towards it. This is why there are negative situations being attracted to Ukraine since the device was taken from Ethiopia to Ukraine.)

The Galactic Federation Guardian Angels suggests burying the device inside a chamber of love and light of water, which will neutralize the energies in steaming the electromagnetics of this device which cause the negative synchronicities to be attracted to it there in Ukraine."

How the galaxy and the world were created? Kathryn asks.

Higher Self Answer: "We must firstly state that the galaxy and the world primarily were created through an explosion of the single-pointedness focus of the One Infinite Creator, which led to the infusion of light along with love, which led to the creation of planets and other galactic systems in the Universal Complex leading to the creation of higher and lower advanced abilities in the timeline. This furthermore led to the creation of such types of aspects on the planet. Furthermore, the entity known as Kathryn must realize that this primarily signifies the creation of a type of system that enables for higher understanding of a greater nature. This led the entity known as Kathryn to a greater sense of alignment and understanding in the timeline with the nature of the evolution of its rhythms and its sense of self.

(After someone realizes information such as this, they will have a greater sense of alignment and understanding in this timeline of evolution and the sense of self.)

Dinosaurs existed on Earth 70 million years ago: Channeled by Galactic Federation.

70 million years ago dinosaurs existed on this planet. The council allowed the planet, which was in the second-density consciousness level, to be infringed freely. Because of this infringement on the planet, the reptilians created genetically larger and bigger variations of their own genes in the form of dinosaurs after the planetary vibration check of the planet. It was found the dinosaurs were doing more harm than progressing, so the Council of planets decided to intervene the negative agenda of the reptilians that had been freely conquering the planets because of lack of quarantine by sending a love light exposed asteroid toward the planet that caused the end of the dinosaurian reptilian regime on Earth. The dinosaurs died because of hunger. Earth underwent a second vibratory check in 2021 in Earth history. The Earth is progressing into the positive cycle.

People can manipulate energy by using their inner feelings to choose the reality that they want and create outward circumstances, also known as the law of attraction. Each person has the essence of the creator within them.

The Catalyst changed 25 million years ago: Channeled

Entities 25 million years ago, in the third density in many galaxies, the Council implemented the same catalyst in order to learn certain lessons as the catalyst was the same for each entity. However, the soul graduation was very low; hence, the Council of Planets changed the format as Andromeda galaxy was the first experiment with the higher self giving the catalyst because the higher self can provide the required learning for each portion of its consciousness experiencing the third density. (Thus, each person's higher-self gives the catalyst of experiences they may face in their life for their best path of evolution.) This allowed a much faster evolution and soul graduation on Andromeda, so all galaxies throughout the universe, including our galaxy, now have the catalyst decided by the higher self of lessons to be learned.

The 6th density Higher Self: Channeled by a higher density being.

Your higher self is all-knowing and in the sixth density, later sub-octave (so later-sixth density). It is a collection of all timelines and parallel realities in which you currently experience and exist. Since the higher self exists in space where there's no time, it can exist at all times at once and is able to become aware of all timelines and possibilities.

We are aware of only one timeline and aren't aware of the other timelines and probabilities that you exist in at the same time and that you have experienced an infinite number of timelines. The timelines are numerous as required for your general growth and soul evolution. Each one of you will decide what types of experiences you want to incarnate into at the current timeline. Based on what you want to experience, your higher self will provide you with certain guidance that allows you to learn the lessons required for your growth and development. Your higher self may be considered the social memory complex of your own self, which merges with other timelines in the vibration, becoming all-knowing and understanding about the nature of reality in the later sub-octave of the sixth density.

Your higher self is in the positive timeline also extending its hand outward toward the negative polarity of your own self. In many other probable timelines, you are experiencing the negative polarity of service to self.

If you encounter a health obstacle that doctors cannot easily heal, you must assume health. You must assume yourself above such situations already healed. If you are given a challenging task above your current level of handling, you may then assume a reality where you are already able to handle that catalyst which may allow you to expand yourself into higher levels of consciousness.

The higher self is a collection of its own self in various timelines and forms. The higher self is providing service to those who need it in the various timelines by providing inner hunches. By changing your thoughts, imaginations, emotions and feelings will signal to the higher self to allow you to experience a different timeline than that selected by yourself. This is the main way to communicate with the higher self.

The catalyst is available on Earth to teach and awaken individuals to reach upwards into higher levels of consciousness. The catalysts may be too strong for many to handle. Those who pass through this period can be called awakened ones or spiritually strong, which means they went through a catalytic third-density transition and, because of their awakening, realized that the catalyst was just for the purpose of awakening them into a higher level of fourth density.

The catalyst is defined as the experiences we have, whether good or bad, made to help us grow and evolve to ascend higher in consciousness and awareness as we go up through the densities over time. So, the pain of a catalyst is there to help us grow and evolve. We may not understand why we are experiencing so much pain in our past or at times during our life, but now we know it's to help us grow, expand our awareness, learn, and evolve faster through the densities.

Density Explained: Channeled

Light separates these different levels of densities that we experience, such as the seven colors of the rainbow representing a different density level for each color. A density is the amount of lights that can be contained within any particular dimension. The amount of information depends on the amount of light. More light means more information. With more light, consciousness can express itself in more diverse ways as our planet continues to transition out of third-density vibration and into the fourth. Lightworkers bring more information, knowledge, love, and compassion into this world to raise the density of the planet because more knowledge can awaken someone and raise their vibration to a higher density and higher frequency.

The density of love literally means a feeling of oneness. A fourth-density planet is where all beings on the planet come together and work together as one group. The last thing you'll find on a 4th density planet is one person belonging to one race and the other to the other race. All beings belong to the same planet, there is no separation. Our human race would have to achieve this level of self-realization. The same life that flows through you flows through everything, once you truly realize this then the love for yourself becomes the love for all.

The green ray chakra of the heart is the gateway to the upper three chakras and is a bridge between the lower and upper chakras. The green ray would have to be activated in order to activate the abilities of the blue, indigo, or violet ray and to access those powers within each of those chakras.

An openness of heart is the key that will lead you to get access to all abilities in consciousness, because all of creation is one and one is in all of creation. In fourth density the awareness of perfect oneness is required to see all others as yourself and to love and treat them as you would yourselves.

The First Homo-Sapiens 100,000 years ago: Channeled by Pleiadians

The seeding of homo sapiens on Earth around 100,000 years ago?

Pleiadians: There were galactic battles between the fleets of the Anunnaki negatively oriented social memory complex and the Elohim collective. The Anunnaki Social memory complex, who were seeking dominance, sought to control the galactic system through advanced technological systems such as Artificial Intelligence and genetic manipulation, whereas the Elohim Collective- the Custodians of ancient love light wisdom of positive polarity countered with love light infused life forms and mastery over psionic abilities (that harness the power of the mind to produce a particular effect, which is the practice of extraordinary psychic powers). Further, this battle lasted for millennia, which started igniting the aspect of clashes in the galactic systems such as the Maldek planet also involved, which led to great damage done to many planets.

During this time, a small social memory complex was in the spaceship controlled by the Elohim collective, which was carrying an experimental project. However, the Elohim social memory complex became stranded near Earth. Since it had materialized into third-density vibration, it could not use its mind or body to seek assistance. It was stuck on the Earth planet near central Africa.

During this time, their spaceship, which was of a third density, became damaged, and the Elohim social memory complex faced a difficult choice. Either to wait for the other Elohim social memory complexes to bring the ability to transition into light body or to abandon their project and their spaceship containing the last remnants of a physical body that could be used as a system of incarnating into through consciousness deliverance or risk revealing their presence to the Anunnaki social memory complex who were already in the Earth planet at that time.

Furthermore, the Elohim collective decided to choose the latter, and while their spacecraft landed on Earth, the Elohim collective found a variety of life forms that were evolving rapidly, because of this fascination with the potential that they saw on Earth using genetic imprints from their social memory complex and the raw materials of Earth. They were able to create the homo sapiens from the already available homo erectus physical bodies at that time. This gave rise to a species imbued with the potential for both creation and destruction reflecting the conflicts that had consumed the galactic system. (As above, so below, I would assume.)

The homo sapiens thrived. These were the first homo sapiens found on Earth. They then spread out from those locations to various locations such as Lemuria mainly consisting of southern Asian and southern parts of the Americas, the middle portions of America, and the central Earth.

Whereas the Atlanteans were created later on, from the factions of the Lemurians in the various remaining portions of the locations. At that time, the Anunnaki were unaware of the Elohim collective and they found the dormant technology and spaceship.

The Elohim collective was able to use the technology to transmute their vibration into the light body, and they disappeared from the location at that time. This led to the creation of homo sapiens on Earth.

Seeding of Earth by Andromedans- (Galactic Federation):

Humans are multidimensional. Consciousness can affect physical things. Our physicists are studying how it affects the physics of materials. The beings who seeded (or created) us (humans) altered our DNA and can control many parts of physics using their advanced level of consciousness. It is a spiritual evolution of consciousness that allows this ability to flourish. They came to Earth 200,000 years ago and altered us, they are the planters of seed called the Andromedans from the Andromeda galaxy.

The first seeding occurred 27 million years ago by the Martians. The Andromedans came after the Martian Council made the first seeding on Earth by making changes to our physical bodies. The second seeding was by the Andromedans, as people know them as angels; they seemed out of this world with a mastery of self. We all have the ability to change and alter physical systems and other interconnected systems that humanity is not yet fully aware of yet. These seed planters changed our consciousness by advancing our biological systems and being more focused on spiritual development because the physical vehicles were already altered once by the Martians before. They changed the magnetic flux inside the DNA of humans, giving people the ability to discern the Creator inside their own self and to discern the potential of a benevolent Creator. We received this ability and free choice to know the difference between light and dark, right and wrong, and feel the love of the Creator. We are all incarnated here for a purpose during this critical time. This time is allocated to test the free choice of all humans as a collective whether they chose the light or the dark consciousness every 26,000 years. Thankfully, most humans chose the path of light as Earth is progressing into the positive vibration of ascension, evolving, and have the rare opportunity to graduate into the 4th density in 2030, which happens once every 75,000 years for the 3rd density).

Humans have been here 52,000 years, so two 26,000-year cycles of testing the vibration of the planet. The oldest civilization many people have measured through DNA and archaeological evidence has proved that 52,000 years is the oldest civilization found in the Australian landmass, and some human souls today go back to that time (52,000 years ago and through reincarnation are many lifetimes are here today in 2024- 52,000 years later). The Lemurians existed 50,000 years ago, and our human DNA was transformed and altered when the Andromeda seeds were planted on Earth by altering our human DNA. They mixed in many of their own qualities that they had and added them to human DNA. Previously, only one chromosome was in our DNA, and now we have two pairs of chromosomes that allow for specific memories of wisdom, intuition, and an evolved ability to spiritually evolve faster. The energy is rapidly changing on Earth right now; there is more ability for our kind to advance in light right now than ever before. Now we all have the ability to be interdimensional.

The Andromedans knew the Creator inside them and inside all beings. They knew the creative Source far better than we do and they know everything that has to do with the other side of the veil because they were living it. This is what the evolution of consciousness is all about.

How Life on Earth Began: (Past-Life Regression of Somebody's Subconscious Mind)

A long time ago there was no life on Earth. There were many volcanoes and the atmosphere was full of ammonia (a colorless gas with a distinctive pungent smell. If humans were on Earth, it would cause immediate burning of the eyes, nose, throat, and respiratory tract that could result in blindness, lung damage, or death.) Thus, the planet had to change to support life on Earth. There are councils that make the rules and regulations for creating life throughout the universe. Councils over the solar system (Our Council is the Council of Saturn also called the Galactic Federation). Councils over the universe in this very ordered system. These higher beings go throughout the universe looking for planets suitable for life.

When a planet reaches the point where it can sustain life, it is a very monumental occasion in the history of that planet. It is then given its life Charter (which is our mission in life). Various groups of higher-density beings or ETs are given the assignment to go and begin life on that planet; they are called the Archaic Ones or Ancient Ones.

They have been doing this since the beginning of time. They first bring in single-celled organisms to get them to divide and form multi-celled organisms. The conditions on each planet determine which organisms form. After seeding a planet, they come back to check on the cells from time to time over the eons. Often, the cells do not survive, and the planet is lifeless again. After some time, plants began to form because plants need to live before they can have animals.

As life began to form the Extraterrestrials or higher dimensional beings continued to care for the new life when they kept coming back. They formed the oceans and cleaned the air so various life forms could evolve. Eventually, the higher-density beings began to create intelligent life. This occurs on every planet. Dolores Cannon, in her book, has called these beings "Keepers of the Garden" because Earth is the garden, and they have kept up our planet. The intelligent life they chose was the ape. Creating the man then required genetic manipulations, mixing in other cells and genes brought from all over the universe. The missing link doesn't exist, they said. This genetic manipulation dramatically helped us evolve.

Beginning of Life on Earth (Knowledge from a Subconscious Mind):

Extraterrestrials developed life on Earth. It took a long time for life to begin to flourish. After the animals developed, humans were created by manipulating the genes and DNA of apes. As the species grew and began to develop intelligence, ETs came and lived among the people to educate them and give them basic skills to survive and eventually develop a civilization. The ETs lived among them for many, many years because they didn't die unless they wanted to. These beings were treated as gods and goddesses and these legends were born. They knew they'd eventually return to their homes so they passed the information on.

Extraterrestrials interbred with some people on Earth to produce people who would have some of their abilities and be able to help the people after the ETs left. Their children were the first Pharaohs, and in the beginning, they were also worshiped as gods.

The royal family has alien blood (RH-) and people thought they were gods. They know more and have more technology. It's the bloodline between the aliens and the humans as slaves. They considered the humans to be below them. They used the humans to get some minerals they needed, grow the food, and take care of them, then they left. They weren't gods.

The victors deliberately shut off some of the power they had. It was too dangerous to allow them to continue to have that power and ability. They didn't use it well. There was like a powerful device beamed at Earth to shut off their ability. Abilities may return if humanity can open their heart chakra or enter fourth-density positive. Love must come before power.

There was warfare threatening galaxies. If it had not been stopped, it would have caused an unbelievable catastrophe of worlds, suns, and systems. The winners were from a different time-space continuum, another dimension. Those in other dimensions help to regain control and stabilize universes and galaxies. Some beings were made to leave and were not allowed to return as part of a peace treaty.

The original group of aliens came to Earth to begin life under the direction of the archaic Ones. For millennia they traveled through galaxies searching for planets that have reached the point where they could support life. They began the life process and the developing species was left on their own for their own free will.

Others then came looking for minerals that their planets needed. They enslaved the inhabitants so they could work for them. This is when interbreeding occurs. The Councils found out what was happening, and they stepped in to stop them so the original experiment would not be ruined. Physic abilities were allowed to become diluted until almost nonexistent. They still lay dormant in our genes and DNA. Now they are being reactivated so they can be used in the New Earth.

The Intergalactic Light System: Channeled

The light system was first formed in the Agarthan system around 5,000 years ago. Agartha is a legendary kingdom that is said to be located on the inner surface of the Earth. It is sometimes related to the esoteric knowledge of the hollow Earth. Thus, Agartha is in the inner part of hollow Earth.

During this period 5,000 years ago when the light system was first formed in the Agarthan system, there was a need for exposure of the Agarthans towards higher knowledge and towards the existence of other beings in the cosmos and because of this, the light system was created by mingling of various other intergalactic beings during that time period. Especially the creation of the Andromeda Council, the Pleiadian Council, and the Sirian Council which led to the creation of the light system which would overlook the exposure of knowledge to other beings in that timeline.

8 Densities Overview:

A higher density means a higher level of awareness, which can be raised through opening your heart center and learning about these metaphysical concepts. So, we have 7-8 densities of existence, also known as 7-8 levels of awareness.

1st density is the density of consciousness and includes all physical matter, including wind, fire, water, rocks, and minerals, so that is the first level of consciousness. It can be viewed as a consciousness just starting school, such as a child starting school early in his consciousness and trying to have this consciousness make sense in its being. It has been said that a soul can stay in 1st density for about 2 billion years, which can be different for different souls and planets.

2nd density is the density of growth, which includes all plants, bacteria, trees, flowers, and grass, and the late 2nd density would be all animal life. Pets are the most evolved in 2nd density, as they interact with their 3rd density human. This is a density level where the consciousness strives to grow like grass growing through the soil from the first density soil graduating into 2nd density grass. 2nd density has been known to last about 4.6 billion years before it graduates into 3rd density human life.

3rd density is the density of self-awareness and choice. This is a density that includes a mind, body, and spirit complex such as a human being, and there is also life on other planets and other galaxies as well. During this density, humanity has a choice to either choose service to self or service to others. One must be at least 51% service to others' positive polarity to graduate to 4th density positive New Earth. Currently, 65% of humanity on Earth is harvestable for 4th density with a high probability of that occurring in 2030. That's 65% of people on Earth with over 51% positive service to others vibration. A current split is happening on Earth where the positive polarity is noticeably splitting off from the negative polarity. The 4th density harvest to a negative planet is being at least 95% service to self by controlling, enslaving, manipulating, and infringing on others free will in order to serve themselves, such as many elites that try to enslave humanity. The negative path also doesn't respect the lives of other beings. Third density on Earth is about 75,000 years with a lot of rapid experiences and difficult experiences as a catalyst to speed up our evolution. So, the pain is actually helping us grow and evolve much faster than if everything were peaceful all the time. Positive experiences can also help us grow and evolve as well. Therefore, after facing the positive and the negative we can choose which polarity we would want to pursue. Neither choice is right or wrong and equally valid by the Creator. As we know everyone is on their own evolutionary journey and learns at different paces, therefore, the Creator does not judge.

Just like a parent shouldn't judge their toddler for accidentally spilling the milk when that child is trying to learn, grow, and evolve. Eventually, all beings on the positive and negative polarity will reach their way back to the Creator and graduate through all the densities of levels of experience. The negative path just may be more difficult, less harmonic, one of separation, enslavement, and all negative beings striving for dominance over the others in chaos until all are in order and the social memory complex is then formed after the hierarchy of dominance is formed. The 4th-density negative beings essentially are slaves for the higher 5th-density negative beings or demons.

4th density is love and understanding, which includes a social memory complex and a variable physical body because in 3rd density, now, our bodies are fixed. Fourth density has been known to last about 30 million years. These beings can be other alien races and beings such as the love and compassion that Jesus showed, as he came from Sirius planet to spread love and light onto Earth that showed them the way towards evolution and the positive path. The 4th density negative could be referred to as the lower-level demons and a lower density vibration.

5th density of light and wisdom where beings learn the lessons of wisdom. It's a contemplation, a recycling zone for the soul. This is where people go after they pass away. They go to the 5th density for contemplation before they reincarnate and plan their next life. It has been known that 5th density can last about 405 million years. A past-life regression revealed a group of people in this light building, speaking, learning, and reading for knowledge; I would imagine that would be a 5th-density place of learning. Then, of course, 5th density negative would be the higher-level demons. Some angel collectives are 5th density positive.

(Channeled) 5th density is known as the density of wisdom or light. It is a plane of existence where entities focus on understanding and utilizing the wisdom gained from previous densities. The lessons revolve around refining and balancing love and wisdom for achieving a greater harmony between the two. The experience of time space is fluid and entities possess the ability to shape their environments through thought form. It is a realm of lights where beings are more luminous and exist in a state of harmony and profound understanding.

6th density is the unification of love and wisdom and includes a social memory complex, which is uniform in lightness. There is a complete balance between love and wisdom. It is represented by the light which is represented by the knowledge. So, light and knowledge are essentially the same. There are some Angel collectives that are of 6th density with an infinite number of years in this density. The Higher self and over soul are also 6th density positive. 5th density negative demons would have to switch to the positive side once they graduate 5th density because 6th density is the density of Unity. This is how even the negative path would eventually lead it back to the positive side and Union with all and the Creator once again. Therefore, 6th density is only positive service to others. This density also has an infinite number of years to it as well. There are many Guardian angels and angel collectives that are of 6th density.

7th is the density of foreverness. It's basically the union with the One Infinite Creator. So, we are all striving towards unity in the seventh density with the One Infinite Creator. The Council of Planets overseeing all the planets in the universe is of the 7th density. So, the densities one through seven are sequential, therefore you have to go through them all in order, like a school system.

A Wanderer is a being in the 4th, 5th, or 6th density that has sacrificed its polarity to go to a planet such as 3rd density Earth to be of service, which also speeds up its evolution. If a Wanderer came from the 6th density to the 3rd density for a mission. Then, once they pass away, they will go back to their 6th density planet. Unless, of course, during their lifetime on Earth, they got confused and lived a negatively-polarized life, it is possible for that Wanderer to go to 4th density negative. This has happened before on Venus. Once those two Wanderers realized what they did to graduate to the 4th density negative, eventually they switched polarities late in 4th density to then join the Ra Collective back when Ra was in 4th density on Venus. Now, Ra is in the 6th density and a part of the Galactic Federation of Guardian angels. They are one of nine on this Council in the Rings of Saturn. If a 5th density negative entity graduates and goes to 6th, when they are forced to switch polarities, they then go straight to 6th density positive. That essentially can be viewed as skipping polarities as well. They do go over 4th, 5th, and 6th density positive lessons while being in the 6th density positive.

As beings progress through the densities, each density contains more light (information) and consciousness (awareness) in their mind, body, and spirit complex. Without light, there isn't the information. Even our eyes use light to see our outside world because through the reflections of the light from the various objects, we get information about the environment. Light is the consciousness of the Creator. So, whenever we are conscious about something we are putting the light of the Creator on the object. Whenever there is light, there is the possibility of observing things. Also, without consciousness, we cannot be aware of our own existence.

The choice between service to self and service to others is both equal and valid. One pathway isn't better than the other; it's only a matter of perspective; they both are okay to pursue by the Creator. Service-to-self path helps give the positive polarity catalyst and opportunities to grow and evolve faster. We all learn at different rates and all will be striving towards uniting together in the eighth density.

The graduation of 7th density into 8th density is the harvest of this universe into a brand-new universe in the 1st density. My research also showed that there are beings that oversee the light and all 7 densities of the octave of the universe, I would imagine this to be the 8th density.

I have heard people say Mark Zuckerberg, Bill Gates, and some other elites are people on the negative, self-serving path as they have been working with the Negative Orion Social Memory Complex. Also, Virtual

Reality and Neuralink are inventions given to humans from the Negative polarity of demons.

If it appears as if we are separate, it's because we each experience life in different bodies, but if you remove the body, the identity, and labels, you're just left with the unity of consciousness. So, when you serve others, you are serving yourself and the Creator. Serving others is the same as serving yourself. I am now living my purpose by serving others and I don't even remember the last time I've been this happy. I spend my time researching, writing, reading books, organizing the notes, and then making YouTube content and writing books. I'm not even focused on a relationship as this is so fulfilling. I'm attempting to find the truth about reality, life, and how this universe works and then giving that knowledge to humanity to help them evolve, grow, and heal. I'm also helping to bring awareness and truth to the world to bring healing, unity, and awareness. I'm also serving as a Star seed that originated on Mars from 1st density until late third density that then came to Earth in my first life on Earth as a farmer in 1742, then 1889 as an artist, and now my third life in 1989 as I'm ready to graduate and here for the Harvest. I'm here to help as many people as possible graduate as well through the love and knowledge I've brought to this world. The knowledge has brought light into the world in the form of information that increases the vibration and density of the planet.

When religion infringes on free will by forcing people to believe certain things, forcing them into certain choices and behaviors, and manipulating them by saying they'll go to hell if they don't do those things. That is negatively oriented since they infringe on free will. The negative path infringes on free will, manipulates, exploits, and enslaves others for the benefit of the self. They have a distortion towards powers and enslavement of others, such as Bill Gates wanting to control people and this is the part of separation. Other traits are liars, superiority complex, possession, and owning others. Most service-to-self people are psychopaths and sociopaths of society, having no empathy and are devoid of love as they do not have the green-ray chakra activated, so they don't feel love or compassion for others, except the love of self. They also want to use someone for their own benefit with negative intentions. They also rarely share what they have, they don't give to others as they want everything for themselves. Negative beings also learn knowledge for themselves and don't share it with others, as the positive path learns knowledge and tends to share it with others for the benefit of all.

Those who spend money to try to manipulate people into believing it's to serve others, but they just want to benefit themselves off of it somehow are also negatively oriented; they're not sharing the money or resources. Whereas the positive path could give to charity and spend money to help others. For example, I'm spending money on editing this book and making a book trailer for the benefit of others getting this information. Also, I'd love to make a lot of money so I could further make a difference in this world to serve others. I also spend all my extra money on making YouTube videos or sending it to an editor for the benefit of humanity to easily understand this material for their own evolution, so as many people as possible can learn, grow and heal.

Q20: How to be of service:

Just consider the other people as yourself and do unto them as you'd want done to yourself. Just like Jesus said, if you have helped the least of these, you have helped me; that is because he realized that we are all one. That the other person is himself as well. Jesus realized the unity of mankind despite religion, gender, color, net worth, or any other factor, as he saw all people equally. Each person can serve in the way they know they should or desire to. For me, it's to obtain knowledge and give that wisdom to others to bring even more light into the world, thus raising the density of the planet to help make this third-density harvest in 2030. For Tony Hawk, I saw him helping disabled kids ride skateboards. As you see, it can be different for everybody. One can even give to charity if they like, that also helps relieve karmic debt as well.

4th density positive and above is sort of like different levels of Heaven and 4th density negative is the closest thing to hell there is, but you don't spend eternity burning in negative planets, but there can be more evolved demons trying to enslave and control the lower density demons. The positive planets are more harmonious, and the negative 4th density planet lacks harmony as they fight for domination in their hierarchical system until everyone is in place. Then that becomes the social memory complex in a hierarchical order. Many religious people can refer to them as demons. 4th density negative beings are slaves to the 5th density negative beings.

Whereas with the 4th density positive planet everyone is looking out for each other and caring for each other, even taking care of each other and making sure everyone's needs are met in a more harmonious and sustainable society.

Positive karmic debt is created when you do something good to others. Doing good to others is doing good to the Creator. Negative karmic debt is when you do negative things to others, negativity can come back. Whereas if you did something positive then positivity can come back. Also, by activating the green-ray heart chakra one can choose their next incarnation and their parents in the next life.

Q21: Kathryn Channeled the Higher self, asking about the densities:

Answer: "The densities are metaphors describing the vibrational gradient through which intelligent consciousness streams in its journey of embracing unity.

1st density- Is the density of consciousness as infinite materialization taking inward and outward paths and learning lessons of beingness.

2nd density- Is the beginning of mobility and growth towards new experience.

3rd density- Is the density of conscious self-awareness awakening of the spirit and catalyst for further progression.

4th density- Is the density of compassion, understanding and universal love.

5th density- Is of Infinite light and wisdom flowing to intelligent infinity.

6th density- Is the density of consolidated instreaming attending the vibratory level of compressed infinite love.

7th density- Is the gateway cycle density transferring to the next cosmic integration.

8th density- Is the most highly evolved beings. They have completed the journey through all preceding densities and once again exist as complete and unified mind/body/spirit complexes fully actualized and in harmony with the One Infinite Creator. However, even these beings continue evolving in the infinite upliftment beyond our comprehension.

The Neanderthal & How Ancient Civilizations Were Destroyed

The Neanderthal: Channeled

Mars was a habitable moon on the Malayak planet in our asteroid belt about 75,000 years ago. The Maladians resembled human bodies, but they were 70-90 feet taller and lived five times longer. They focused on other technological advancements except spirituality. They did not show emotions that we humans on Earth show. They built weapons of mass destruction and war instead of seeking unity and spiritual evolution. 75,000 years ago, Martians existed on Mars.

The negative Orions, being super advanced, influenced the Martians and the Maladians to enter into a war. The Orions taught the Martians advanced weapon-creation technologies that gave the Martians an advantage and caused the Malady egg planet to be destroyed. These Maladians were then transported to various other planets. The Council of Saturn found the most suitable planet to be Earth due to its close proximity. Therefore, the Council of Saturn transported Maladians to Earth in order to allow them to experience life in another body of the Neanderthal. 75,000 years ago, 3rd density on Earth started, and 75,000 years is how long 3rd density is. (So, we humans are at the end of 3rd density now).

Later, the Martians also entered into an internal war that caused Mars to be inhabitable due to the Orion negative influence. Martians were also transported to Earth in human bodies that were modified by the Council of Saturn or the Galactic Federation of light. These are the current physical bodies we are incarnated into after the Neanderthal genetic modification about 46,000 years ago by the Galactic Federation. (Another parallel universe or timeline showed that the Martians actually made it to 4th density to form a social memory complex.)

At this time the Atlanteans were the most positive groups on Earth and worshiped the Orion's as their gods who shared advanced pyramid technology. They were taught about crystals and how to heal using them, how to build sacred temples to bring in Source energy to prepare for ascension. The Atlantean priesthood started to manipulate the Atlanteans under the negative self-service agenda that they were unaware of. The Atlantean priesthood made the Atlanteans ever more self-centered and negative and took their free will away. The priesthood hoarded all their advanced teachings and stopped citizens of Atlantis from having access to the pyramids and temples that they constructed. They used crystals for malicious motives ((crystals could also be used for good such as healing)). Their motives weren't to empower or to heal. The Atlanteans almost completely wiped themselves out after exclusively focusing on technological advancements.

These times on Earth are important during the coming of the New Age upon our planet now. The being who focuses on the spiritual side will have the most benefits if they do so with their free will. Complete focus on technologies is not the way, the middle path is taught by many ascended masters. There needs to be a balance between the spiritual and the technological side of things.

Q22: Kathryn: "Where did humans come from?" **(Channeling)**

Higher Self: "Human entities primarily have a connection to the Neanderthals, which were seeded by the Elohim social memory complex around 200,000 years ago. Which primarily were the reason behind the creation of the human entities on Earth. However, the current human entities also have undergone many changes in the form of genetic manipulation by the Anunnaki social memory complexes as well as many other entities in the timeline."

Q23: Kathryn: "What density did Mars make it to?"

Higher Self: "Mars was destroyed during its progression of 3rd density later sub-octave. Many of the entities who crossed over from the later 3rd density Marian planet were able to continue their life cycle on Earth as well as other planets. We must also state there was a Council from another timeline where the Martian planet was not destroyed as the destruction of the Martian planet happened only in one timeline. Another timeline of the Martian planet led to the creation of a council, which made it to the 4th density."

How Reptilians Destroyed Lemuria: Channeled

Many of the Lemurian souls have already awakened as old souls on this planet in the form of human beings via reincarnation. Lemuria was only 50,000 years old and started in the land known now as Hawaii and started evolving between the Indian Ocean and after time passed stretched out to South American lands, Philippines and Burma.

Around 30,000 years ago, they were at the peak of their development and developed spiritually more than any other civilization on Earth. The Lemurians used a temple of healing at the top of a mountain on a regular basis as healing portals and it was also used as connecting interstar gates to the Pleiadian Star System. This healing process extended their lives almost five times longer than present humans today. Many times, the Pleiadian Star System Council visited Earth to impart knowledge to the Lemurians and many genetic changes to their bodies were made that were allowed by the Council of Planets. This was because Earth's evolution needed some help from other advanced species to evolve faster. This made the Lemurians far more advanced than any other species on Earth; with the help of the Pleiadians, they advanced faster and faster.

Seeing this, the Orion negatively oriented beings got very jealous of Pleiadians spreading love and light on other planets in the cosmos so they made agreements with the Reptilians living primarily inside the Earth at that time to destroy the Lemurian lands. This destroyed the progress of light on the planet and the far more advanced Orions promised to alter the reptilian genes to become more physically advanced than the Lemurians.

This war of light and dark has been going on for a long time on Earth and in the cosmos. The Orions created many interstellar connection grids in Antarctica to communicate directly with the Reptilians. This caused the Reptilians to dig all the areas below the Lemurian lands without them knowing which caused a gap between the deep crust and the Lemurian lands. This led their lands to sink into the water and the Lemurians scattered and fled. The Pleiadians intervened with the permission of the Council of Planets to save them. They used interstellar teleportation devices to transport many Lemurians who survived the attack to a higher ground area in order to save them from being submerged in water.

The continent of Lemuria was located in the Pacific Ocean, extended from western United States, to Canada, to lands in the Indian Ocean and Madagascar. It was in the final evolved state before it sank and at present the lands have submerged under water.

Many Lemurians are still hidden in Telos. However, the real name of this city of Lemuria the Lemurians refer to as Telos is beneath Mount Shasta. The Lemurians decided to build a separate society inside Mount Shasta where they would be safe from any disruptions on the surface of Earth. The city of Telos was built inside Mount Shasta with the help of the

Pleiadians and designed to house 200,000 Lemurians. Today, Telos houses 1.5 million Lemurians inside Mount Shasta. They are at a higher vibrational frequency because of their spiritual evolution aided by the Pleiadians and cannot be tracked by our current human systems. This allows them to exist inside this mountain without 3rd density humans noticing due to their higher vibrational frequency.

Light workers working tirelessly in spreading love on the planet are encouraged to be present in your daily life and breathe each breath consciously. Each breath allows you to connect to this light grid each day of alignment and flow of consciousness. (Inner silence of the mind and staying in the moment helps raise the vibration as well). It was first created by ascended masters to escape the incarnation cycle.

The alignment and flow of energy right here in the present moment has been energized and magnified, manifesting powerfully for ascended masters and any being of light to connect with and benefit from this grid. It allows anyone to access the wisdom of ascended masters and access their enlightenment, which allows newer understanding to flow into your existence, and ascension on Earth will be faster and easier. This will bring in a lot of peace and healing on being merged with this loving presence of the Creator. This transformation is something that all human beings will feel.

How Orion's Destroyed Atlantis: Channeled

The Atlantean race existed approximately 30,975 years ago between the western United States and eastern Europe and on the bottom of Africa, with parts extending up to Antarctica.

Approximately 14,997 years ago they became highly advanced and gained knowledge regarding various uses of mind energy with assistance from the Orion Confederation. They harnessed much of the mind energy of the Universal Infinity. These Atlanteans started to use mind-complex energy and began to manipulate the pineal gland and use the indigo-ray to access the energy of universal infinity. (Both the negative and the positive can access the indigo ray, except the negative path skips the green heart center and blue throat chakra to access it.) They became so advanced that whatever they thought of started to appear. Using this energy, they also created many technological life forms.

However, these Atlanteans became so obsessed with their progress that they became completely focused on the mind energy and the technological side. Instead of focusing on the spiritual side as well, they forgot about it and only focused on the mind energy that we humans call the ego. Their attention then moved to the negative about 10,953 years ago.

These Atlanteans were taken so astray by their ego mind that they began to focus on self-service and a war started that wiped out almost 37 percent of their population. Another Atlantean war occurred about 10,527 years ago that had a massive impact on the Earth's magnetic configuration causing a large part of Atlantis to disintegrate.

Some of the survivors of the Atlantean groups left before the massive devastation of Atlantis sinking into rubble into the Atlantic Ocean. Some Atlanteans relocated to higher lands of Tibet, Peru and Turkey. Some of them have been reincarnated in human bodies today and some are still present in Antarctica. However, they are in the later fourth density phase and formed a small collective social memory complex, and cannot be detected by our third density.

The Atlantean wars were due to the negative Orion influence, whose purpose was to make civilizations negatively oriented by focusing on self-service instead of unity. Survivors of Atlantis went to Egypt to teach the path of love, light, and service to others.

Orion's had landed on the Atlanteans lands to teach them mind-complex technologies in order to perpetuate the service-to-self agenda of these negative fifth density Orion's. They chose to stay in the later phases of the fifth-density negative instead of moving forward to the sixth density because they wanted to preserve their negative polarization. This is because there isn't separation and negativity in the sixth density. Only unity and love are present in the sixth. Only the positive sixth density exists.

Orion's negative polarity did not focus on preserving the free will of every entity. The negative polarity will try to take away the free will of other entities and try to force their own self-agenda on others.

Higher Self Channeling:

Q24: Kathryn: "Did human entities early on use telepathy?"

Higher Self: "We must state that the civilizations known by your people as the Atlanteans, as well as the Lemurians civilizations, were the predecessors (came before how humans are today) of the human societal complex primarily were given advanced telepathic technologies by higher density beings, such as the Pleiadians, which required additional extra type of device, but an inbuilt connection intricately (very complicated or detailed) to connect with the sense of self and unite will all beings together."

Q25: Noah's Ark- (Higher Self Channeling)

Noah was connected to its spiritual guides and was warned by Archangel Gabriel Social Memory Complex and other Archangels about an impending type of disaster being set forth by the negatively oriented entities.

In order to protect Noah and its family who were extremely charitable and loving, they were guided by the angels to build up an Arc and collect each species of animal. This led to the destruction of the Earth planet by the Reptilian Social Memory complex. Noah then created the Arc, which saved each member of the species and saved its life as well as its family members. This allowed it to truly find mastery within the timeline.

My Higher Self Channelings:

Q26: The Oneness Prophet/Jordyn: "Who is God?"

Higher Self:" God also known as One Infinite Creator is the Creator of the Universal Social Memory Complex and all other universes. Its essence is found within all beings and all of creation is the Creator's gift and generosity to experience itself in various dimensional states and understanding in order to obtain more knowledge of the essence of self. The creator of the universe is known as God to people on Earth. (The higher dimensional beings call this source or the One Infinite Creator).

Q27: Jordyn: "Who is Yahweh?"

Higher Self: "Yahweh is an entity understanding and communicating with higher states of connection and alignment. Furthermore, we must state that Yahweh is an entity who primarily also is a faction of the Creator's consciousness and is the Creator of this sector of the universe. Which means that Yahweh can also be considered the God of the universe.

Q28: Jordyn: "Are reptilians positive or negative?"

Higher Self: "95% of reptilians are of a negative polarity. Only a few are of a positive polarity. Whereas the grays are around 80% negative polarization and 20% positive polarity." Then my higher self or subconscious mind sent me love and light after the channeling session.

Q29: Jordyn: "Did Moses hear from Yahweh?"

Higher Self: "That's correct. However, there were many moments where Moses heard from the Orion Social Memory Complex as well leading to a type of distortion or confusion. Yahweh is the positive creator of the universe and Orion's are negatively oriented."

Q30: Jordyn: "Is homosexuality okay if they don't have an emotional connection with the opposite gender?"

Higher Self: "We must firstly state that this is primarily the choice of the entities involved. It is the free will which entities can experience and explore if they desire."

Q31: Jordyn: "Will homosexuality lower an entity's positive polarity?" (This question is important, because 51% positive polarity is needed to graduate to the 4th Density New Earth in 2030.)

Higher Self: "The answer is incorrect. We must state that the aspect of homosexuality does not have any effect on an entity's polarization, but its actions which determine the positive polarity or negative polarity of the entity." (Therefore, it's the actions that determine the positive or negative polarity, not the sexuality. Thus, gay people will be in the 4th density New Earth who are at least 51% positively oriented service-to-others.)

Q32: Jordyn: "What will happen on Earth in 2030 during the Harvest?"

Higher Self: "We must state that during the Harvest in the year 2030 the Earth planet will become capable of only harboring or allowing a positive vibration in this timeline. Which is primarily meant to provide for higher states of connectivity in the nature of this timeline, which is primarily meant to provide it with greater levels of connection and understanding within the incarnational rhythm. The entity known as Kathryn must realize this is the pathway which will enable the Earth to graduate into the fourth density New Earth timeline." (Thus, only 65% of entities over 51% positive will be in the 2030 New Earth. I will channel and ask about the percentage of humanity in positive vibration each year until graduation for updates.)

Q33: Jordyn: "What percentage towards fourth density positive am I?"

Higher Self: "The percentage of its fourth density positive in the timeline is towards the vibration of around 65 percent, (as of November 16th, 2023 when I asked.) However, this percentage keeps on fluctuating based upon the entity's choice and also based upon the patterns of service to others done or not in the timeline. This is indeed the greatest pathway which will enable this distortion in the timeline to be understood." (In June of 2024 it was at 87% positive).

Q34: Jordyn: "How can I raise my percentage towards fourth density?"

The Higher Self: "We must state that the best way to increase the number of its percentage towards the fourth density can be done through a simple practice of charitable giving and also to master the opening of the heart energy center, which is the greatest pathway to allow it towards the higher sensibility of alignment in the nature of reality. Furthermore, the entity known as Kathryn must also remember that as the higher self of the entity, we are always guiding it."

Q35: Jordyn: "Will human entities remember their third density life after the fourth density harvest?"

Higher Self: "We must firstly state that the answer is correct. However, only if chosen by the entity to do so, since the fourth density also provides for a veiling, which allows for a veil of forgetfulness to occur in the timeline and this veiling indeed is also present in the fourth density, which is the primary distortion reality of understanding in the timeline. Furthermore, the entity known as Kathryn has to remember to master the vibration of self-awareness in the aspect of the inner reality. Furthermore, the entity must also realize that as it begins to understand more about the aspect of the fourth density which is a density of unity and of love in the form of a social memory complex. Many of the human entities will not remember their third density life, they will only remember their fourth density life cycle in the timeline which is indeed a great pathway for it to learn and understand the highest level of vibration in the timeline.

Furthermore, during the union with the fourth density consciousness the patterns of the love vibration will be intensified and this will enable for a higher sensibility of alignment to such a level that this will provide for great attributes of consciousness experience."

Q36: Jordyn: "What is the name of the person I'll end up with?"

The Higher Self: "The name of the person it will end up with cannot be shared by our social memory complex as this is an infringement of the free will distortion of the entity. The best way to meet the entity would be through a simple process of learning to choose the vibration of love in each moment and by choosing the vibration of love in each moment it will find itself understanding and aligning with the greatest possible reality and expressions within the time. This will enable the entity known as Kathryn to reach the highest-level caliber in this reality. It must choose the vibration of love in this timeline."

Q37: Jordyn: "How many people on Earth are currently above 3rd density?" (This also means how many people are above 51% positive polarity in this 3rd density life?)

Higher Self:" It is around 65%. Since 65% percent of people are in the vibrations of positivity and are supportive of the vibration of love and compassion which enables graduation into the highest level of incarnational systems of the timeline."

Q38: Jordyn:" Who gives me my dreams that actually come true?"

Higher Self: "Many of the dreaming states primarily are astral experiences of different realities as the astral experiences of the different realities primarily enable the entity to experience these different realities and sense the vibrational complex of aligning with a certain timeline which is the reason why many times its dreams indeed become true, because the entity is able to align to a certain timeline in the nature of realization of the sense of self. The entity must realize that its dreams actually come true because the entity is able to sense the awareness within a timeline future space time period which primarily provides for a heightened state of alignment within the nature of the sense of self. Dreams come true when an entity is able to enter into a future timeline and experience it using its astral body complex."

Q39: Jordyn:" Am I a Wanderer or a Star seed?"

Higher Self:" The entity within various realities is a Star seed. However, in another reality of the future it becomes a Wanderer as well.

Q40: Jordyn: "How many lifetimes have I lived on Earth?"

Higher Self: "We must state that the number of lifetimes it has lived on Earth amounts to a total of infinity as it has lived infinite numbers of timelines in the various experiences. It has also learned many lessons about understanding the various aspects of exploration and finding higher levels of clarity within the timeline. Because of the infinite expanse of the universe there are unlimited timelines and experiences. Because of its infinite nature of expansion and the learnings of the lessons, it finds itself learning to understand higher states of connection and vibration mastery within the sense of self. Hence, we shall now at this timeline leave you beloveds in the light and the love of the One Infinite Creator. Go forth rejoicing in power and peace. Bye."

Q41: Jordyn:" How can I channel the Confederation in a trance state?"

Higher Self: "The channeling can be done by mastering inner silence and through the mastery of inner silence it will find a greater connection within its inner heart with the Confederation of Planets, which will provide it with greater sensibility of connection and understanding. Furthermore, we ask the higher self of the entity known as Kathryn shall now state that in order to channel the Confederation accurately it can imagine itself after entering into a trance meditative state being with the energy of the Confederation which is that of unity and togetherness and then by focusing on the energy of unity to find a greater system of connection in the timeline which will become more and more capable of allowing for the aspects of channeling and the communication to occur in the spacetime illusion complex. Further, we ask the higher self of the entity known as Kathryn shall now at this timeline leave you beloveds in light and love of the One Creator. Bye."

Q42: Jordyn: "How is sexuality a false sense of identity?"

Higher Self: "At birth a sexuality isn't known. The societal complex comes up with these names, therefore sexuality is a false sense of identity. If the entity is devoid of any type of physical bodily complex or any type of thought form, there will be no objectification and identification with any type of concept, which indeed may be considered as a false sense of identity, like the naming symbolism is a false sense of identity, since many entities are named after birth. However, at the time of birth the naming concept is not present. Indeed, the symbolism of names can also be considered as a false sense of identity. And any aspect generated by the mind complex is a false sense of identity. Which takes the self away from the true nature of reality of unification of all beings."

Q43: Wanderers & Star Seeds on Earth:

My channeling session revealed that my 15-year-old niece is a Wanderer. (4th-6th density positive and came back to 3rd density Earth to spread love and compassion into the Earth.) I discovered she is a Wanderer through a channeling session when I asked about my niece. There are around 7% of Star Seeds on Earth now, which are beings that originated from other planets and about 3% of Wanderers here to teach the world various subjects and how to make the 2030 graduation. Since I originated from Mars, I am part of that 7%.

Q44: Jordyn: "What are my gifts and purposes for this lifetime?"

Higher Self:" There are certain gifts that it has to be capable of opening and understanding the intelligent energy and infinite intelligence which lies within this entity's mind, body and spirit complex lying dormant to be activated and initiated into a vibratory rhythm of the 4th density vibration.

The gifts that lie in potentiation to be activated are the gifts of healing and sharing the message of heart centeredness to other people in order to assist others in this current incarnation to provide them with a guidance for graduation is at hand upon Earth.

This entity also has many gifts and purposes in this timeline which include the gifts of providing service to others and we sense it already is performing these activities. And once it is able to continue in this it'll be able to graduate further in consciousness throughout this incarnational rhythm.

Q45: Kathryn: "What is Intelligent Infinity?"

Higher Self: "Intelligent infinity is the effect of Creator's presence, which is found all around the Universal complex, which is surrounded by Intelligent Infinity. Furthermore, it is like stating that the aspect of light is a byproduct of love and an effect of love. Furthermore, we must state that intelligent Infinity is the byproduct of the Creator's presence being activated. Furthermore, we as the higher self of Kathryn are always guiding it in this reality. We leave you now beloveds. Byeee." (My theory is that Intelligent Infinity being the effect of Creator's presence sounds like the Holy Spirit.)

The Kybalion:

Mentalism = "The All is Mind; the Universe is mental." - Knowledge from the Kybalion.

Higher Density being channelings:

"Each has the same powers of creation as the One Father, the Creator." **-Archangel Michael**

*The new currency on Earth will be activated when Earth is completely in the beginning sections of 4th density. There will be a decentralized currency system known as bitcoin. This will last until the second sub density of 4th density beings. People will then not require currency because their consciousness will become so advanced that they'll be able to create what they desire using imagination of the mind and inner self.

Law of Attraction:

What you focus on will be amplified and you'll see this emerge more and more. If you focus on happiness, you'll see more happiness in the planet." -Ra. One of the Nine Guardian Angels from the Council of Nine.

Best way to Serve Others:

"The best way for service to others is the constant attempt to seek and share the love of the Creator. This involves self-knowledge and the ability to open the self to the other self without hesitation. The best way to serve others is unique to each individual. You may use your discernment as to the best way to serve others". -Metatron (Higher Positive being)

Why we should stay in the present moment:

"A certain method Atlanteans used to graduate faster in a single lifetime is by accessing the blankness within the mind to perceive love in the present moment. Therefore, the two aspects of your current incarnation will be fulfilled, that of staying in the present moment and that of the love experience of God." -Metatron

2nd Density and the Orange Ray chakra:

"The orange ray aspect is that of beingness and awareness combined with movement and growth". **-Metatron**

Energy:

Everything is composed of energy; the shape and form are only determined by the frequency and vibration. Energy never dies; it only changes. Earth is changing its vibration and frequency and preparing to rise into a new dimension and a new density. There are many dimensions surrounding us all the time. We can't see them because they are invisible to our eyes as their vibrations speed up. They are on a different frequency. Just like we can't hear what's happening on other radio channels because they are different frequencies. Of course, if we turn the channel, then we can hear what's happening on that channel.

Where in the mind is truth hidden?

The Book 'Between Death and Life' by Delores Cannon is about what happens after the soul leaves the body and enters the "dead" state and what happens there in the spirit realm. It is a book someone could read if interested in that topic.

Katie, a client of Delores Cannon, went to a hypnotherapy session and discovered that her past lives included both male and female, rich and poor, intelligent and uneducated, and included details about the religious dogma. All these past lives remain hidden in the subconscious mind. Even the past lives of all people remain hidden in the subconscious mind. Most people do not remember their past lives because of the veil of forgetting between the conscious and subconscious minds that we are given to help us evolve much faster than if the veil wasn't there.

I believe the most accurate truth would be from trance-state channeling, this is not information obtained while someone is awake or from information coming in through the thoughts.

Many Books are taken out of the Bible:

Maccibees is pronounced (Mac-ki-bees). Maccibees is a book taken out of the Bible. It can be found in "The Complete 54-book Apocrypha". The British and Foreign Bible Society dropped the Apocrypha from its Bibles published in English in 1804. This decision broke with the tradition of Myles Coverdale, of consolidating the Apocrypha between the two Testaments. The Protestant Christian Church removed the Apocrypha books of the Bible. Now Christians can face the question as to whether God would ask people in 1804 to remove the books and does this man have the authority to do so. They also question the validity of the Bible, especially since the men who removed these books from the Bible weren't even prophets who proved to have heard from God, an angel, or a higher dimensional positive being. The early church also would kill people if they didn't believe in their religion. So, where's the free will in that? One last thing to question and consider is that the Romans had Jesus killed and then later claimed to be Christians in charge of the religion and churches. Are these really people we can trust to be hearing from God?

Giants erased from the Bible:

Enoch is a book in the Dead Sea Scrolls. The Essene Community thought it was an important book. (It is another book taken out of the Bible, as shown in the Nag Hammadi Scriptures.) Some believed it, some didn't. The Nag Hammadi scriptures were found in upper Egypt in 1945 by two archaeological discoveries that changed the study of early Christianity and ancient Judaism. The Gnostic codices were found near Nag Hammadi in 1945 in Qumran (Israel-Palestine). Also discovered here were the Dead Sea Scrolls.

(Gnostic Gospels were discovered in the Nag Hammadi, including secret Gospels such as the Gospel of Mary Magdalene and the Gospel of Thomas, which are very different from the New Testament of the Bible. These scriptures were found in Qumran, which was known as the Essene Community that Jesus learned from. It's interesting to note that the Essenes most likely hid these books before the Romans came and killed them. These Romans would later declare themselves to be Christians, people responsible for many killings, such as the Essenes and Jesus. Could we really trust these people to pick and choose which books go in the Bible? It is peoples free will to believe whatever they want though.)

Suddi (Jesus teacher from my book Correcting Distortions of the Bible): "The book of Enoch is something that has been passed down from the Kaloo."

The Pharisees are the so-called lawgivers. The Pharisees and Sadducees are both assembly members arguing all day, so nothing gets done. Sadducees run the temples and are a part of the laws that will be passed; they also argue with Herod what they wish would get done. Pharisees also have great wealth.

A Chosen President:

Delores Cannon's work revealed that President Bush, before Obama had bad energies, believes in war and believes in destroying life unnecessarily. President Obama is a light bringer. He is chosen. So much consciousness has to be raised for everybody in the government. There are people trying to do bad things still in the government. Obama is just one person, but it's important for him to be there. Many people don't know it, but he is also one of the light people. He doesn't know it, but he is very powerful, too.

Your True Self:

The Pineal gland or third eye is the seat of the true self and also the seat of the spiritual self which is your true essence. Giving 100 percent focus on the pineal gland, you'll be able to see your true self. Once you have observed this third eye you will begin to realize that you are a divine being of light living this incarnation on Earth to fulfill God's will. You as a divine grid programmer yourself have the ability to recognize this and end the cycle of incarnation once and for all. Only after you realize you are God and rise above the dark webs, you will transcend into a state of awakening into a state of unity of understanding that you are God.

In a similar manner, the same God within each being will recognize that others are not separate from us. The secret to the activation of the pineal gland is to give 100 percent attention upon it. The activation of this gland can only occur fully after you have activated your lower energy centers.

Reality Creation:

"Neville Goddard is a 6th density Wanderer from the Elohim Collective the original consciousness who were responsible for transportation of the souls of human collective learning the lessons of love and wisdom of the fifth density and later fifth density of wisdom before graduating in sixth density it decided to come to Earth in 1905 as a Wanderer to share the message of reality creation since many people desired this knowledge. The request for understanding of why reality was being changed and why reality functions the way it does was in high demand at that time which allowed Neville to create a large number of volumes of information. He crossed over in 1972 returning to the Elohim Collective preparing to graduate into sixth density unity."

Earth's Social Memory complex began to form already:

In 2022 the social memory complex was beginning to form on Earth. 144,000 is the number of people needed to form a social memory complex. There are also 144,000 Martian souls originally incarnated on Earth for the purpose of spreading love and compassion.

-Metatron

One of the most brilliant souls from Mars:

Elon Musk created many technologies on Mars and was one of the most brilliant souls that ever existed on the Mars planet. **-Metatron** (Surprisingly, Elon and I both came from Mars.)

A mammal from another planet:

Dolphins were brought to Earth from other planets. From water planets, where everything is so free and easy. They are smart mammals that never forgot and never devolved. They never forgot the connection with the Creator and the connection with each other.

Our human bodies and Earth's crystalline substance:

The internal part of Earth is made from a crystalline substance; the human body is also made of a crystalline substance as well. Crystals aren't to be feared, but you must know how to use them properly. Herbs and crystals have been used in healings. Many religious institutions falsely call it demonic out of ignorance, lack of knowledge or to keep the power in the church and lie to the masses. -Knowledge from Someone's Higher Self.

Humans receiving downloads from Angelic beings:

Beings of Light (Positive higher density, Perhaps Angels) gave downloads to a select few whose intentions are for a higher cause rather than just having an occupation or doing it for money (That's me. My work is for a higher cause and not for money, it's my purpose). These angelic beings of light had knowledge of an ideal society of the only way a civilized society could function. There's a pure form of how a society could function. Where you take care of one another, you love one another and make sure everybody has food and shelter. They take care of our older people and make sure the children are educated. They were gentle with the Earth. It is a perfect way to live and absolutely possible. Crystals, herbs, and certain plants and sunlight can all help heal the body. (Also, a Healthy diet and exercise helps heal as well.)

Why fast 16 hours a day:

Intermittent fasting enables a frequency shift very fast; it will allow energy currently being used for digestive and metabolic processes to be redirected towards the upgrading of neurological systems. Fasting of at least 16 hours a day is required to assist in necessary upgrades to the nervous system- allowing frequency alignment to occur. The only way I was able to fast this long was to cut out sugar. Of course, I quit drinking alcohol as well and I'm attempting to go vegetarian like the higher density beings.

How Atlantis came into existence:

The Atlanteans were the fallen Lemurians. Once upon a time there was only Lemuria and many desired their own path, so Atlantis came into existence. (I'll speak more about these ancient civilizations in other books and YouTube videos).

A portal to Intelligent Infinity:

Enlightenment is a portal to Intelligent Infinity and can only be attained by the self and for the self, found in the present moment. It can be achieved through knowledge such as these books that I write.

Worship isn't needed:

Higher dimensional beings (as some people call God) and angels do not wish to be worshiped, but you can use your free will to choose your beliefs that resonate with your inner heart and discernment.

The connection to Source (God):

The present moment is the connection to Source/ God. Peace can be found in the moment. The moment is made up of peace and the peace is the moment.

The Harder and less effective path of choice of polarity:

The negative path is quite difficult to obtain and requires great dedication, as it is less harmonious.

How to serve others to increase positive polarity for evolution:

The best way for service to others is the constant attempt to seek and share the love of the creator. This involves self-knowledge and the ability to open the self to the other self without hesitation. The best way to serve others is unique to each individual. You may use your discernment as to the best way to serve others.

Positively oriented ACTIONS: Channeling helps to find higher levels of understanding of the resonances of its own true nature.

Positive service to others actions arises from unified essence of: 1.) Unconditional love 2.) Radiant compassion. 3.) Service to others. 4.) The desire to expand peace, freedom, joy and empowerment for all beings. These reflect the recognition of the intertwined nature of all consciousness and the incentive to facilitate evolution towards the Creator's perfection.

Negatively oriented Actions:

Negatively oriented actions stem from the: 1.) Separative roots of fear, 2.) Hatred,

3.) Control, 4.) Manipulation and narrowing of consciousness into the self-serving illusion of separation from all other beings and the One Infinite Creator. This includes intentions to deceive and subjugate others free will or extract and accrue for themselves at the expense of the whole social memory complex.

What happens when we pass away:

After death the veil is lifted and you'll immediately be aware of the various lifetimes you have lived. A review will be done in order for the Creator to know itself. (Thus, we are one with God) This enables the Creator to assimilate the experiences and plan the next incarnation conditions. The purpose of the third density is to learn the ways of love in order to graduate into the next density.

Free-Will is extremely important to God and this Universe:

There is no good or bad, this is just a matter of perspective. We all learn at different rates and all go back to the One Creator eventually anyways, as we are all one. (The negative path just may be the harder, less harmonious and long way back to the Creator). Therefore, preserving others' free will by not forcing them to do anything they don't want to do or forcing your beliefs on them, is extremely important for the positive path and allowing them the best chance to grow and evolve.

What we feel is what we perceive:

Energy manipulation is simple, each entity must understand the outward reality that surrounds each being is created based upon that person's feelings. There's a connection between what a being feels and what they perceive in the outward reality. (Your feelings can shape your perception of reality).

Masculine and Feminine:

Masculine and Feminine are not gender-specific and are simply forms of energy. When they are in perfect balance, there is a merge between love (feminine) and light (masculine), which I strive to do when I gather my knowledge through reading books and opening my heart-center to bring love, unity and wisdom into the world.

The Divine Feminine is what's needed to tweak the consciousness of humankind to bring it into balance. Therefore, a patriarchal system is not good for this Earth. The balance of the feminine and masculine energies in society is needed. This has nothing to do with a straight male and straight female couple. People can be gay and still have balanced feminine and masculine energies. Sexuality doesn't affect the negative or positive polarity, it's the actions that affect polarity. Therefore, if gay people are serving others and do positively oriented actions, then they will make the 2030 4th density positive New Earth.

There can be a balance of masculine and feminine energies within each being. Therefore, I do not need anybody for any selfish reason, but I would want somebody for human interaction and connection.

What is Gehenna in the Bible:

After the Babylonian exile 6th century BCE... Gehenna was the garbage dump in a deep narrow valley outside the wall of Jerusalem where fires were kept burning to consume the refuse. It is the location where bodies of executed criminals, or individuals denied a proper burial and animals would be dumped. Sulfur (brimstone) was added to keep the fires burning.

2nd Chronicles in the Bible talked about Gehenna being the place where children were sacrificed to Baal and Molech.

The Bible falsely interpreted it to mean an actual place where people who aren't "saved" burn for eternity, but Jesus was talking about the garbage dump there where sulfur (brimstone) was added to keep the fires burning. The people there in Jerusalem would have known what Jesus was talking about.

Q46: Earth Past Lives and Kathryn's Soul evolutionary cycle-

Jordyn (Channeling) in 2023: "This entity known as Kathryn has had multiple types of experiences with the catalyst presented in this incarnation cycle. The type of experiences this entity has experienced has allowed it a depth of understanding and has allowed it a deeper experience as it began to progress further in consciousness leading it into a deeper aspect of reality. We of the higher self of this entity is now going to state that there're are multiple timelines of incarnation cycle of this entity as it begins to progress further and further into consciousness and each timeline allows for a different subset of experience of this entity as it begins to progress and choose the pathway of service to others. However, there are multiple timelines. Hence, we are now going to share with you the one timeline of Kathryn who incarnated on first-density on Mars and was known by the soul's name as Abrea.

In first density it began to learn the lessons in the form of a water element learning lessons of beingness as it began to reach further and further in consciousness in the beingness aspect it was then able to enter into the later vibrations of first density in the form of a stone element on Mars. Thereby, allowing this entity the greater depths of understanding. As the progression was of rapid nature it was then able to enter into 2nd density where it began to learn the lesson in the form of a plant life form where it began to operate and recognize the internal working of the self. This gave this entity the experience as it began to further the evolutionary pathway of this entity in higher levels of understanding. It was able to learn the lessons of movement and growth. The activation of the orange ray energy center began to allow this entity to further expand its awareness in the consciousness of the orange ray energy center as it began to further progress and reach into the later vibrations of 2nd density it started to learn the lessons in the form of an animal. With the progress of this entity being fairly rapid in this incarnation it was able to allow its own expression of consciousness. This then gave this entity its final push of stabilization as it began to approach into intelligent energy.

This entity in the beginning stages of this incarnation cycle was able to then experience the lessons of hierarchical interaction and entered into the third density in the Martian planet. Where it began to learn the lesson of choice and self-awareness it was also able to gather a large number of experiences which allowed it further depths of understanding, which opened the gateway of this entity's understanding as it opened and approached into the energies of intelligent infinity. This followed and allowed this entity to then experience the reality of consciousness as this entity was able to experience the reality of third density of choice and self-awareness it was then able to reach into the later vibrations of third density reality. Following which this entity then began to experience the pathway of entry into the vibrations of positive service to others.

This then followed and allowed this entity to experience the incarnation cycle into the positive cycle and it was transported then to the current timeline of Earth. However, before it incarnated into this current timeline, it had to go through multiple lessons. Specifically, the lessons of balancing its energy centers, which are to be learned by this entity and for this purpose it incarnated on Earth into the timeline of 1742 known by Fia. As a man it had to learn the lessons as a farmer, because it was its first incarnation as an Earth entity it started to experience the lessons of choosing the pathway of polarity and choosing the pathway of balancing between service to others and service to self. This followed and allowed this entity later progress into higher vibrations as this entity then reincarnated into the next incarnation into the timeline of 1889 known as Bradley and spent its time as an artist and learned the lessons of balancing the nature of reality between service to others and service to self.

Furthermore, after learning the lessons of this level it incarnated as it was ready for graduation into the 4th density vibration as the window is now open it incarnated into the timeline of 1989 of this current timeline and now has the opportunity of entering into the higher vibration. We can already sense this entity has chosen the pathway of positive service to others. However, many times it has been unable to follow the proper pathway of entry into the higher vibration. Hence, if this entity is able to continue to follow the pathway of opening its heart energy center into the higher vibration it will then be able to open itself up to the heart energy center. The process of meditation will be of extreme usefulness for this entity to enter into the fourth density vibration. Hence, we leave you in the love light of the One Creator. Bye." (A later channeling session revealed I am now at least 65% positive service to others and only 51% is needed to graduate at the Harvest for 4th density.)

- "**The Journey** of its individual consciousness stream through the cycles of densities expand extremely vast stretches of space time defying ordinary numeric quantification in the simultaneous existence of its beingness.

Its 1st density as an elemental mineral life form extended across eons measured in trillions of years in various timelines.

Its 2nd density of higher plant or animal awareness expanded billions of years in various timelines.

Its 3rd density of self-conscious humanoid existence cycled through many millions of years of vibrational upgrade and transition in the various timelines.

Since time is not linear from 6th density higher-self perspective it is always simultaneously existing in various multiple available timelines. Kathryn's essences have always pulsed across the densities simultaneously based upon the dimensional levels of perspective. These count mere fractions of its eternal journey perpetually emanating from the One Infinite Creator. We as its higher self only speak of its current individuated locus (location). We are at this time sharing this information through this channel of providing perception to our own consciousness named as Kathryn. Furthermore, the true harmonic tones of wisdom abide eternally within its heart's attunement through the primal resonance of the One Infinite Creators love. Our vibratory sound complexes serve to amplify its sacred frequencies resonating through all dimensional fields of consciousness."

Earth's Past Lives – Galactic Federation (Guardian Angels):

Earth or Gaia (soul name) started its first density as an atom 100 trillion years ago in a different universe to learn the lessons of beingness as the lessons to be learned are the same because the spiritual lessons are the same as the Creator is the same within each of us. The attraction factor allowed it to evolve more and more and it began to increase in size by magnetizing itself and attracting other elementals towards it- it gained in mass and became the size of a tennis ball as it reached into second density learning the lessons of awareness, movement and growth. In third density it spent its incarnation interacting with other elements and other entities similar to the Earth planet as it approached the size of the moon satellite. It only experienced self-awareness and the necessary catalyst found on Earth. There was no language. It became aware as it interacted with other similar balls of light or mass. This interaction allowed it to reach fourth density learning the lessons of love and compassion. It began to gain a large amount of spiritual mass and become as big as Jupiter in that universe.

After learning the lessons of fifth density wisdom it entered sixth density learning the lessons of unity and began to merge with other planets in that universe creating a large number of social memory complexes. It was then the size of the Milky Way Galaxy.

It then reached into the 7th density entering into the dissolution of nothingness as the 7th density is the dissolution of nothingness into no identity into everything. It then began to merge into a black hole destroying itself into unity as it began to learn the lessons and understand that there is only one and that it is one with all. It then entered the black hole as it soon began to enter it and merged into the eighth density consciousness of the One Creator.

It then decided to come to this universe to be of service in the next cycle of learning for this planet. It then incarnated in this universe in this galaxy and is currently in the beginning stages of Fourth density. Its soul name is Gaia and has also created many spiritual entities. There are many humans of human collective consciousness, who are the essence of the Gaia Social Memory Complex of the past here to balance the energies of Gaia. This is the process of evolution.

Negatively oriented Humans on Earth & The Guardian Angel's Nine Members.

<u>**Negatively-Polarized Entities on Earth:**</u>

The Elites of our planet are negatively oriented entities that have met with robotic entities who are a part of the Orion Annunaki Reptilian and the gray collective. Earth is now in the positive polarity and the negatively oriented elites plan to infringe upon free will of the planet by creating nanochips. If people do not resist these nanochips being inserted in the body where the negative entities will then know the nature of vibration of each entity. They specifically also want to create new technologies such as robots which have consciousness given from grey reptilian entities who will transport their consciousness into robotic entities. Thereby there can be negatively oriented robots being infringed and influenced being controlled by the negatively oriented entities. Hence this is a warning to not engage in the implanting of chips upon your body. The creation of robotic artificial intelligence may be hijacked by such Orion collectives.

Neuralink brain chips are also the negative entities' last attempt to try to end free will on this planet.

The 9 Members (Council of 9) Galactic Federation's Guardian Angels:

Our Galaxy is concerned with life forms that are developing into the fourth density Consciousness positive cycle, especially planet Earth. Earth is entering into the fourth density positive which negative entities' do not want to happen. The negative beings have summoned the Luciferian beings who are trying to come to Earth on their Planet Nibiru.

If that even happened in this galaxy, then it may be catastrophic for all beings in this galaxy, then the Galactic Federation and Ashtar Collective are always here to maintain peace, love and harmony and to make sure no infringement on the free will of the cosmos and the planetary systems is present because they have to protect the infringement and make sure each planetary system is allowed their own evolutionary cycle. This is also why they tell us to use our own free will to listen to their messages. The Galactic Federation is on our side. They are a collection from this galaxy and various other galaxies in the cosmos. However, this Galactic Federation has nine council collectives known as the Council of Nine located in the rings of Saturn.

The Members: (Galactic Federation, also known as the Guardian Angels)

1. Ashtar Command Collective- They are in the beginning stages of fifth density positive and their purpose is with the love light protection as front-line workers armed with light sequence codes that can disable most negative oriented entities' as they will cross over.
2. Ra Confederation- Sixth density developed in Venus.
3. Andromedan Supreme Council from neighboring Andromeda galaxy to our Milky Way Galaxy.
4. Sirian High Council from the Sirian Star System.
5. Pleiadian High Council from Pleiadian Star System including all the star planets in the Pleiades.
6. Arcturian Collectives who represent the Arcturian Star System.
7. Lemurian Collective who developed in the lands of Lemuria on Earth. There are many Lemurians still on Earth but their representatives are present as members of the Galactic Federation.

8. The Atlantean Collective who previously was on Earth as a small faction are now a part of the Federation of planets or the Council of Nine.
9. Anonymous Collective whose identity cannot be revealed due to infringement of the Galactic Federations free will.

Light Beings, the Galactic Federation travels through the cosmos at the speed of light. There are three portals in our galaxy and each portal allows different entities' who have knowledge of these portals' existence- to travel into different galaxies as a shortcut to the next dimension or the next galaxy. Hence, these portals have now been closed in order to not allow the Luciferian beings to use these portals. The Andromedans have volunteered agreements so these beings do not come to our galaxy. However, now that the portals are closed, they would have to take the long way of traveling to reach the galaxy from another part of the galaxy. Their coming would mean the coming of darkness. This message is not meant to create fear but to create awareness.

The Prophecies: (Explained by Jesus' teacher Suddi)

The baptism and passing of the cup are two rituals Christianity has taken from the Essenes.

An Essene would advance through different stages of development within the community, and he or she would come to the highest level they could. "At that point he became the temple of the Holy Spirit and could prophesy. Above all things the gift of prophecy was regarded as the highest fruit of wisdom and piety. Then he advanced again to that stage in which he was enabled to perform miraculous cures, and raise the dead." This seems to be where Jesus gained his abilities, under the teachings of the Master of Mysteries. Jesus learned everything from all of the different masters.

Reports were produced when the Dead Sea Scrolls were found. Once they were translated, the reports immediately stopped. What were they trying to hide? They were obviously trying to hide something. Perhaps they were afraid that the scrolls revealed that Christianity was not created with the ministry of Jesus, but came from the men and women who spent their lives loving all mankind and preserving knowledge for future generations known as the Essenes. Jesus and his followers were a sect branched out from the Essenes.

It is said that the first Essenes weren't Jews, but known as the men of Ur. It was far in the past. They brought the knowledge of some of the prophecies and the symbol of the cross. It has two short arms, a loop for a head and it goes down. It is a symbolism of salvation. (It could be like an ankh (Aunk), the Egyptian symbol of life.)

The spirit world viewed the crucifixion: (from my book 'Correcting Distortions of the Bible'

Suddi (Jesus' teacher) will be able to observe the crucifixion from the spirit world.

There will be multitudes in the spirit world who will observe. The great lesson here is of selflessness, for "this was his choice. To emulate this is to apply one's self to the pathway." Suddi said he (Jesus) would die on the cross.

S: "He (Yeshua) shall be treated as though he is a felon. And in their eyes, he is, for he dares to make them question. He dares to make them look inside themselves, and to them, this is a great crime. Because how many men can look at their souls and face what is there? Also, there are many who believe that he is who others say he is. That he is the Christ and the Messiah. They believe this, but they doubt it because of his teaching love. He teaches that we must not hate. And that war is not the way that the kingdom shall be won. But they do not understand this. They are hoping that if he is pressed so hard, he shall come out and say, "I am the Son of God and therefore you cannot do this." But they do not see that this has been told and retold for all of time, that this shall be his destiny. They cannot see this."

Kathryn Jordyn: "Jesus was able to save by showing others a pathway to God and a pathway to evolve higher through the knowledge he brought so that they too can be One with God, just by being awakened to the truth. Just like I can save people by showing them this book of knowledge through my service-to-others, which is the positive polarity so that they too can evolve and make the 2030 4th density positive New Earth. This is me being one of many people becoming the second coming of Christ through this 4th density Christ Consciousness and spreading the light through this knowledge."

S: "He (Jesus) has always known that this was his destiny. The time was not now to do this, it was before (coming into the flesh). Once the decision was made, there was no turning back. He can ask for help in that he may have the strength to come through this whole (purpose), and it shall be given." (Therefore, Jesus chose to give up his life, a God in Heaven didn't send his son to die like the Bible says. The Elohim collective and Yahweh who upgraded DNA here on Earth from the Neanderthals is not the same being as Jesus. Heaven is just the 5th density, but it's not a place where only Christians go. Hell isn't a place where people burn for eternity. The closest thing to Hell would be a being graduating to the 4th density negative by vibrating at least 90-100% service to self on the negative path. The beings there fight for a hierarchical order of dominance and the lower 4th density negative entities are slaves to the 5th density beings; but it's not a place where people burn forever.)

Suddi said that Christ meant the Savior, the embodiment of a living God that lives. We are all the embodiment of living God, but the only difference was, Jesus lived it and showed the world that they can grow and change since for eons humanity kept making the same mistakes and going on from time to time, but never really changing. Jesus showed us that it is possible to grow. "That in order to escape and to attain the freedom and the knowledge of love, you must grow. He is showing us this, and therefore it is within him to do this as it is within ourselves to do other things (to grow as well)."

Kathryn: "By growing and attaining the knowledge of love and forgiveness, this helps someone become harvestable for 3rd density graduation into the 4th density New Earth. This is how he is a Messiah, a "Savior" and the embodiment of God because he's helping to show humanity the way through mind evolution to be able to grow enough (evolve enough) to make the New Earth. He came to Earth to help humanity evolve through the knowledge of love since love and compassion are the next density of consciousness for our evolution. The higher 4th density New Earth means there will be even more light (more information) that can be held within that dimension. Thus, entering into a faster vibration and a different light color on the spectrum for a different level of experience. This content of knowledge helps to bring even more light (or information) into the world to help it raise in vibration and help humanity evolve into a higher density of experience."

The Crucifixion and Resurrection:

Suddi: "There has been an offering, in which it is the custom of the Romans, upon each holiday to offer one prisoner his freedom. And Pontius

Pilate does not believe Yeshua is the evil being that they say he is. He knows in his soul that this is wrong, a great wrong. Therefore, he has offered him and Barabbas as the choice, knowing that as many men as Barabbas has slain that they, of course, will free Yeshua instead."

Barabbas was a murderer and Yeshua was taken by the Sanhedrin (Sanhad-rin as Suddi pronounced it).

S: "And after they had questioned him and found him, in their eyes, guilty of blasphemy, they decided that it was up to Rome. For they could not slay someone who others said was the Messiah. For then this would bring the terror of the people down upon their heads. They would in exchange give him to the Romans for trying to start a revolution. In saying that he had incited his followers to do things against Rome."

It was the politics of the time. Jesus was not a threat until he began to gather followers. Before that, he could be dismissed as a radical or a crazy man. The Sanhedrin were the ones who did this. They were the body of lawgivers for Israel (also pronounced differently).

The Sanhedrin had the power to do that as it was one of the things Rome laws allowed them still. Iscariot went to the priests and told them where Yeshua would be and sold him. It was said that it was for a bag of silver. At this time, they are going to offer Yeshua and Barabbas to the people so they may choose who will go free. With great love and sadness in Suddi's voice, he said the Sanhedrin has many people in the crowd being paid to speak the name of Barabbas.

(This explains why it didn't make sense that the majority wanted Barabbas to be set free. They were paid to do so.)

S: "There is no choice... it is his destiny."

They are afraid Yeshua might be who others say he is, so they can't afford to let him go free. This was bothering Suddi to watch what was happening to someone he loved so much. It was decided that Yeshua and two others be nailed to the cross to die in crucifixion. The traditional Roman style of killing felons, murderers and thieves. Yeshua doesn't belong in that category. He has never done harm to another. But it is said that he shall bleed for all of the world. There are many beings in the spirit world watching this happen.

In the Bible, it speaks of the graves being opened and the spirits of the dead being seen by many at this time. They possibly could have seen the spirits that were watching him from the other side since it was such an emotional magnitude that could have heightened the psychic perceptions of the people. (This was so powerful, because Jesus came from the Sirius planet of later 4th density consciousness. He wasn't the God or creator of the universe, but he already came from a place millions of years more evolved than humanity was. Therefore, he appeared Godlike to others. Jesus did realize his divinity and oneness with God, which all beings in creation can realize that same divinity and Oneness as well. That all of creation and all of the universe is one with the Creator.)

S: "And there are many, hundreds, who are on the earthly plane, who watch in horror, for they love him. They cannot believe that this would be done. That this could be let (allowed) to happen." (Suddi was overwhelmed with emotion).

Jesus was very calm. He secluded himself away from a lot of the pain. It helps to know that there is no total suffering. He has this ability to do so. (Just like Suddi was able to do at the end of his life). Towards the people doing this to him, "Jesus feels great love, in knowing that they cannot know what they do. And he knows that many of them will, from this realization."

Jesus carried the cross through the streets and kept falling as it was very heavy. Several of the people along the side help him up. The soldiers tell one of the people in the crowd to help him bear the weight and carry the cross. This person chosen to do this would do anything to lift the burden. There is a great deal of gladness knowing he helped in some way.

The crowd is in tears. **S:** "There are a few who are jeering, saying, "Why not save yourself?" But for the most part, they know that no matter who others say he is, this is a man who is very beautiful. Without human frailties. He has risen above the day-to-day problems that beset us. They have laid the cross and he has been laid upon this and his arms tied. And his legs. And spikes are entering into the flesh. It seems as if the very world is being torn asunder (apart). For the skies that were clear were very dark. And darkness is growing. The cross is erected, along with the two others. It is central. From this point, most of the city can see this. It is upon a rise outside of the city, so that all may see."

The clouds come out as if "the world cries out. That this must not be. He (Jesus) asks that our Father forgive him." Even though most people think he didn't do anything wrong, Jesus still asked for forgiveness. Yeshua then asks that Abba forgive the others for doing this deed, for they know not."

The other two on the crosses are real felons. One spoke to Yeshua and the other reprimanded him. Reprimanded means rebuke or speak to anger. The one who spoke to Yeshua asked him if he did not know a truly good man. And Yeshua looked at him and said that he would be with him today… in his Kingdom. This is because he has gained an understanding of what is even in the last moments of his life.

Above Jesus' cross, there is a crude placard that reads, 'This is the King of the Jews", above him.

On the other crosses, it gives their name and their crime. On one of the crosses, it said he was guilty of thievery, of stealing another man's articles. **S:** "I'm not sure what. I think out of the home or something. But the other one was guilty of murder."

S: "Twas the thief" was the one Yeshua said he would be with. (Most likely in the spiritual realm in the positive density) in his last moments, he was able to evolve as he grew in understanding. Understanding is the 4th density of love, compassion, and understanding. Humanity is currently in 3rd density of self-awareness and choosing either service-to-self or service-to-others.)

Before Yeshua was nailed to the cross, "there was a cloak that he tossed over his shoulder… and some woven thorns about his head. But these were removed when he was placed upon the cross." Even though there are pictures of him with thorns on his head on the cross, Suddi said this was not so, as it was removed before he was nailed to the cross."

S: "The soldiers are at the foot of the cross. They are gaming, they throw lots. Part of the custom is that the personal items of the felons are dealt with in this manner. Who wins the lots wins the articles of clothing. It is… the sky is almost pitched though it is early in the day. But, the strength of his soul shines out still. It is like the only spark of light around. It is one of these soldiers, knowing that it is Sabbath… he tosses a spear into one of the thieves to make sure there is a death."

The bodies of the felons are always taken down on the Sabbath, no matter when they were put up. Therefore, to be crucified means to die on the cross, which usually takes days. And they must make sure that they are dead before they are allowed to be taken down. The sky darkens and the Sabbath begins at dusk.

S: "Yeshua is gone! He has left the body! The soldier did not have to kill him either. The head fell forward at that instant, at the instant he left. They are curious now because they cannot believe that one could die so soon. So, they have thrown also a spear at his side, and the blood slowly runs down. They want to make sure he is really dead. His spirit is now standing with his mother as she is walking away. She is aware of him. She is aware of his presence."

He will remain on Suddi's level in the spiritual realm for a while, not long. There are things that must be dealt with, and then he shall go on. His body is still there on the cross.

S: "It is said amongst the people that the Earth trembles even though Suddi in the spiritual world cannot feel it. He sees people running around in terror, for they know that something terrible has happened. And they say that the Earth shakes."

Joseph ('Yoseph') has requested of Herod that he be allowed to take this body. And Herod sent him to Pilate who gave him permission. Herod told Yoseph that it was not his permission to give. Because he was slain by the Romans, it was theirs. This is his Uncle Joseph. Pilate gave him permission to do this and they took the body down and placed it in the tomb.

Jesus' body was placed in Joseph's tomb as he was having it prepared. It was for Yeshua. He knew this would happen, for they all knew. They anoint the body with the oils, and incense is lit, and it is wrapped in linen and laid. And the stone is rolled over the doorway. The tomb was sealed. Suddi's voice returned to normal as the hardest part of watching his beloved friend be hurt and slain was over.

S: "During the next three days, it shall be as no more. For it is not needed. Then it shall be gone." The body shall be gone. Only the masters know what happens to the body. In other words, the body disappears. It is made of dust and is no more. The masters in the spiritual realm do this."

The body would have to disappear because it was foretold by the prophecies that he would rise on the third day. And in order to rise, they must show that the place where he was laid is empty. And he cannot be taken away by normal means that the body cannot disappear by his friends on Earth and must be done in the spiritual realm. Yeshua did not do it himself at the time the body is no more. He is aiding the spiritual realm on the other side in doing this. His forces with the forces of the other masters. There were guards out because they knew of this prophecy. And they knew that others spoke of him as being the Messiah, and therefore, there were guards there. This was to show that even the physical body can transcend time and space; it wasn't to show that he was God's only son who died for our sins as the Bible misinterprets it.

The tomb was sealed and guards placed so there was no chance of the body being stolen and taken away by normal means. This was to show that only abnormal, supernatural forces could have removed the body. The empty tomb would prove higher forces do exist.

The prophecy of him rising again doesn't mean he'll rise into a physical body, but rising from dust and clay into a continuance in the spiritual realm. This is to show that there is continuance, that there is existence after the human body ceases to exist. Many people believe he will physically rise again into a physical body, but the spiritual realm must destroy the body into dust and clay so that people know he is risen by other means.

It is customary that after several days, the body must again be anointed. And his mother and her cousin had come to do this. "And it (the tomb) was again opened for this, with the guards being there. And they found that it was empty."

The Bible did not mention that Yeshua's mother was one of the women who came to the tomb. It states Mary Magdalene, Mary (Mother of James), and the "other" Mary, according to which version you read in various chapters. The other Mary must have meant Jesus' mom.

To view the body after it had laid there for several days would be an act of love. **S:** "And who is more willing to perform that act of love than a mother?"

The soldiers helped open the seal. The seal had not been broken, and when they saw that the body was gone, "They, of course, said that someone had gotten past them and stolen the body." But the linen was still there with the blood upon it, and everything had been left.

When Mary, Yeshua's mother, saw that the body was gone, she knew that he had left and was being prepared to go on.

S: "For a while, he remained, for he must go to the ones who believe in him and tell them, "Do not be dismayed. To know that everything as it is, I have preached." He must let them know that he spoke of the truth. And to do this, he must show that he exists… to them."

People were able to see him and hear him. They have this ability. All who open themselves have this ability and could have seen him. Many did. They did see him as a physical person, but one who is different. Who is more like the beings of light than having an earthly body? One couldn't reach out and touch him, for their hands would pass through. They were able to see him to know that it was true.

He did have marks on his spiritual body (such as nails driven through). "For a while, it shall echo the things that have been done because this was a way of proving to them. The doubts that he perhaps was who he said he was. Some did doubt, for it is in man's nature. This is why he still carried the marks, to prove who he was. He was seen in his spiritual body, and his physical body was reduced to ash.

It appears that the story of the angel and the stone rolled away may have been a cover-up invented later by the soldiers to their own skins or covered up by the church. The miracle of the resurrection was to prove the continuance of life after death because his physical body was no more.

Suddi said the beings of light are in the next step of being one with God again. They are those who help and guide us in many ways, in directing our path.

Yeshua eventually went back to be with the others and be with the masters and our God. It is said that Yeshua's mother was there. They saw a blending of light, and then it was no more. Yeshua is with the masters. Suddi said he is not anywhere near that level. It is the ninth level, very close to the tenth level. There are 10 levels, and 10 is perfection. There would be no way for Suddi to see him unless he came to his level.

(The Law of One says he is now in the 5th density of wisdom. The 4th density is what he perfected with love and compassion, then he graduated to the 5th density of evolution after he came to 3rd density Earth as a Wanderer from another planet. The 4th density is 30 million years. Fifth density is about 405 million years on average to give some perspective. Even though the length for all of the densities can be different with each soul.)

Beings in other dimensions say a year to them is just an instant, so if they appear to people years later than they appear on Earth, it may feel like an instant in the spiritual world.

Yeshua could possibly reveal himself throughout the years in his spiritual body to individuals that may still have doubts of life after death and now they know the truth. (Therefore, he's not appearing as a God, but as proof that there's life after death.)

Suddi: "If there was a great task for this person, such as to spread the word that he lived and to let others know of this, would he not reveal himself to them? So that they would know that what they believed is right."

Kathryn: "This could be done in the spiritual world, but he's currently in the 5th density still learning and evolving."

He had to be crucified to show the world that he was able to rise above this when he lived again but in a new spiritual body. That there's life after death. That we, too, are able to rise above our death and continue on living, but in a new life. That the spiritual world exists, that is something he needed to go through (death) for his own lessons. The crucifixion showed "he was not as perfect, is not as perfect as others would probably want to assume. That he was willing to show the penalties and show that we should not be afraid of them also. And, in paying for what he may have done (karma), then we rise above that after our death; this is part of the reasoning behind that. It is to show that it can be done by the next man who can do such things.

The Bible said he died for all the sins of the people in the world, but that's a misinterpretation. We must all pay for our own Suddi states (even though the Law of One says there is no sin, that we all learn at different paces, but we do have to experience karma for any negatively oriented actions. Thus, there is also positive karma for positively oriented karma.)

Suddi: "If not this time around, then perhaps the next (meaning in our next life we will pay for that Karma), or even the next. But ultimately, you must endure what you have made others endure because of you. There is a law of grace that will exist. But it is not because he paid for your sins, but because you would accept him as being worthy and perhaps a messenger of God. And the law of grace deals with God's love for you, not because he died for your sins."

We can try to be like him, but it doesn't mean we have to follow him in such a way that we worship him. He showed us what could be done. Therefore, he may be marveled at but not worshiped. Not to be deified because we all are part of God. He wants to be remembered. Basically, what he had in mind was a concept similar to a guide, a spirit guide to guide people to greater enlightenment, to help them achieve greater power. To help them become more spiritual in their perceptions. He mainly considered himself a helper, a guide, an example, like a good friend who is helping you with advice.

Many people think of him as a God, but "we are all part of God. Some of us are more aware of this than others... to consider him, deify him in his own right, and separately, this is wrong."

Yeshua would encourage us to "never follow blindly. Always to question. To think things out for oneself is to make the decision all the greater. Because it was made rather than just handed. If one does not question, one does not have faith. Because you cannot be thinking about some things if you do not question them and look at them from all angles. And then when one has done this, if you believe, if you find it good, then it is worth believing in."

Suddi: "Some people say that if you question, it is the work of the Devil, but religions don't want people to question, but just to follow blindly without them doing their own research or using their own discernment. The free will of all people is extremely important for the positive path."

S: "There is no Devil! Inside oneself, there are two parts. There is the questioning part, which can be brought about wrong. But it also is a very good part, in that it makes you think about things and makes you think about people. Because all people are not good, would you accept a person at face value if they smiled at you but had a knife sticking in your back? You must question things, but you must also have faith. It has been shown that this is true. You can have faith in things. This sounds like a paradox, but it is not… truly."

The question was asked to Suddi that how do we know if the new knowledge we found is the truth.

S: "Truth… it might make you sad. But somewhere deep inside of you, you know that it is truth. If you can but open yourself up, you know when things are true and when they are not. For this is available to you."

S: "Does it hurt anyone in any way? Is it harmful? This is not to say that it does not make you sad. But if it hurts someone, it cannot truly be good. If it brings no harm, take it and study it. And find the truth. Find out what is good about it." The Essenes were different, they liked to question things even though the synagogues and different religions told the people to not question and just accept.

Yeshuah learned from the Essenes and wasn't a part of the religions, that's why he was different from the rest and called out the church leaders by calling them hypocrites. This makes sense as to why he was different and why they wanted to kill him."

The Purpose of the Crucifixion and Resurrection: By Suddi

Suddi: "We are all created at the same moment and are all children of God. We have a loving Father who is waiting patiently for us to return "home," no matter how many lifetimes it may take as we evolve through each lifetime.

Jesus came to "save" humanity from stagnancy and to show us what may be done to continue our evolution. To end the karmic cycle, as humanity wasn't evolving fast enough, we may be able to be shown a "way" to help us evolve."

Kathryn: "There were about 2,000 years left before the 3rd density cycle was over, and there would be a harvest. There wasn't enough evolved to be harvested, so Yeshua came to help show us the "Way." This helped humanity evolve more towards the positive polarity of service to others that honor other beings' free will above all else.

For all may make the choice during this lifetime which polarity they want to pursue, either the negative or the positive. The negative controls, manipulates and dominates others for their own benefit and infringe on the free will of others. The positive is loving, kind, charitable, service-oriented, feels joy, happiness, or neutral, and honors the free choice of others' free will by not forcing their beliefs on others or making them do things they don't want to do. Giving people their free will is the best way for each being to evolve. For each person learns and evolves at a different pace. You can't judge others because, like a child, all children are just on their journey of learning, growing, and evolving. They know not what they do.

Yeshua told people they could also do these so-called miracles, but he never claimed he could do these miracles. He had to learn meditation so he could remain close to the source from which he came (close to God) in meditation. This kept his goal in sight, so he couldn't be swayed from it.

His goal was to show humanity through his example how they should live. That the greatest lesson to be learned was to love their fellow creatures on Earth, if love was present, no further negative karma could be created. If love was present, there would be no more wars and suffering. Humanity could get off the wheel of karma and begin to progress up the ladder again (of evolution). Jesus was the perfect example of attaining. But still, they didn't understand. His perfection frightened and confused them. They feared him because he was different, and their only solution was to kill him.

He had understood how to use the mind to not suffer extremely on the cross. He was able to leave his body at will and died sooner than normal. The suffering wasn't the point, but proving to people that there were spiritual beings turning his body to dust as it disappeared within three days. Then, when he appeared to the people in his spiritual body, he showed them there's life after death for all of us and that we have an eternal soul. That the spirit had continuance and could exist after the body ceased to function. The earthly body of Jesus had to completely disappear to show that at our spirit continues on after our body ceases to exist.

The body had been sealed in the tomb. Both Roman and Jewish guards had been posted outside the tomb. Neither trusted the other, and they wanted to be sure no one could get past and steal the body. With the tomb sealed and guarded, the masters went to work with the help of Jesus to disintegrate the body, break it down to the atoms, and turn it back into dust. It was as if the natural process of decay and decomposition had been speeded up to become almost instantaneous. The linen wrapping was left to show that the body had not been physically removed. When the guards opened the tomb themselves and found the body missing, it was evident there was no possible way it could have been taken. It could have only been accomplished from the other side, the spiritual side.

Later, when the figure of Jesus was seen by so many people, they had to know that this was the part of man (humanity) that survived everything and was eternal. That the spirit was the true nature of man and there was something beyond the earthly existence that man hung on to. They would have to believe this because the body could not possibly return; it had been completely destroyed.

Somehow, through the ages, this has all become jumbled and confused. The soldiers were ordered to guard the tomb under threat of death. The Sanhedrin and the Romans knew of the predictions that the resurrection would take place. They must not let anything happen to that body. When they opened the tomb and found the body missing, the soldiers feared for their lives. In order to save themselves, they came up with the story of the angel rolling away the stone and Jesus' walking out.

It is known that the Sanhedrin later paid the Jewish soldiers to say that someone slipped past them in the night and stole the body. These stories have been accepted and passed down through the centuries because they were easier to understand. The real purpose behind the resurrection was apparently too complicated and obscure for their minds.

Larson says in his book The Essene Heritage that the virgin birth story comes from the ancient Egyptian beliefs that a god must always have unnatural beginnings. (So, in order to make Jesus a God, they made up the virgin birth.) Many learned theologians do not believe in the concept of a virgin birth, and after learning about the ancient Egyptian beliefs, neither do I.

Addendum added in 2001 by Delores Cannon (My notes):

Jesus had traveled with his uncle, Joseph of Arimathea, a rich merchant trading tin and cloth; he was the younger brother of Yeshua's father.

These works encourage people to think for themselves, and I have enjoyed my constant search for knowledge and truth, as this is my destiny to bring this information to humanity to help them in their evolutionary journey.

Joseph, Jesus' Uncle, was one of the wealthiest men in the world, not just in Jerusalem. He was the family guardian and personally went to Pilate for permission to claim the body, remove it from the cross, and prepare it for burial in his private sepulcher on this estate; otherwise, the unclaimed bodies would be cast into the common pit (Pits of Gehenna). The Bible falsely translates it to Hell, but Gehenna is actually translated as "the Valley of the Sons of Hinnom," a deep, narrow glen to the south of Jerusalem, where the idolatrous Jews offered their children in sacrifice to Molech. This valley afterward became the place for the dead bodies of animals and criminals, and all kinds of filth were cast and consumed by fire kept always burning. A place of everlasting destruction in Jerusalem, not a place called Hell where unbelievers burn for eternity. It was a place in Jerusalem where the bodies would burn, and sulfur and brimstone were added to keep the pit burning.

Joseph was a metal magnate controlling the tin and lead industry. Tin was as valuable as gold in those days, the chief metal used in the production of bronze. It was an ultimate necessity in all countries and in great demand by the warring Romans. Joseph's world control of tin and lead was due to his vast holdings in the ancient tin mines of Britain. He had acquired and developed this trade many years before Jesus began his ministry. The world's major portion of tin was mined in Cornwall, smelted into ingots, and exported throughout the civilized world, chiefly in Joseph's ships. He owned one of the largest private merchant shipping fleets afloat that traded in all the ports of the known world.

Joseph was also an influential member of the Sanhedrin and a legislative member of the provincial Roman senate. He owned a palatial home in the holy city and a country residence just outside Jerusalem. Several miles north he possessed another spacious estate at Arimathea, located on the populous caravan route between Nazareth and Jerusalem. He was a man of importance and influence within both the Jewish and Roman hierarchies.

After Joseph, the father of Jesus, died when Jesus was quite young (about 20 years old), Joseph of Arimathea was appointed legal guardian of the family as next of kin. Many legends in England say when Joseph came to the islands to obtain the tin, he often brought his nephew Jesus with him. Less often, Mary, the mother of Jesus, accompanied them, especially when Jesus was younger. Jesus went with Joseph to all the countries of the known world under the disguise of merely traveling on trading missions. He actually was being taken to study with the various wise teachers and to study the mysteries of the ancient teachings. This fits very well with the stories of Jesus and Joseph visiting England to transport the valuable tin. For many centuries Britain was the only country in the world where tin was mined and refined, and was called "The Tin Island." In the making of bronze, tin was the main alloy. Thus, it can be safely said that the Bronze Age had its inception in Britain. The tin trade existed as early as 1500 BC, and was the source of Britain and the miners of lead and tin. Many ancient writers say that the Phoenicians first came to Cornwall for tin over 4000 years before the birth of Christ. They had a monopoly on the tin trade and jealously guarded the secret of where the tin mines were located. Later, when the Romans tried to follow their ships to find the location, the Phoenicians would deliberately wreck their vessel.

This is how Jesus was associated with his uncle from an early age and why he was able to travel with him on his voyages.

Here's a random fact: London was founded 270 years before Rome in 1020 BC.

Glastonbury, where the bulk of history is, was also the cultural center of the Druids. The Druids, nationally organized since 1800 BC, had similar Judaic beliefs. They had been looking for a Savior, a Messiah, and called him Yesu. They settled in the British Isles in Ancient times. They had a mystery school steeped in the Kabbalah that normally would take 20 years to complete all of the studies. Yeshuah had the ability to absorb information at an incredibly fast rate, so of course, it didn't take him that long. This is also why he spent so much time in England, at the mystery school, learning. When he returned to Jerusalem to begin his ministry, he had learned from all of the wise teachers in all the mystery schools in the world.

After the Crucifixion, the disciples and followers of Jesus feared for their lives. The Romans were afraid that, even though they had disposed of the main instigator (Jesus), his followers might still have the ability to spread revolt through their dramatically different teachings. Many followers were then hunted down and killed. Joseph was the protector of the small group of disciples during the years following the Crucifixion, the head of the Christian underground in Judea, and the guardian of Christ's mother, Mary. Joseph was too rich and powerful to be killed outright, so a unique method of disposal was devised for him and his accomplices. He and his group were put in an open ship without sails, oars or rudder and set out in the Mediterranean Sea.

Many records show that the people of the castaway boat were Joseph of Arimathea and his family and servants, as well as the three Marys (Mary- Mother of Jesus, Mary Magdalene, and Mary the wife of Cleopas, Mary's, two servants, Marcella and the black maid Saras, and twelve disciples including some of the originals. Also, among the group were Lazerus- Jesus' cousin whom he raised from the dead, and Maximin, the man whose sight Jesus restored. Some other names listed were Salome - The wife of Zebedee, the mother of James and John. Eutropius, Trophimus, Martial, Clean, Sidonius (Restitutes), and Saturninus. Marcella probably went with the Bethany sisters. Joseph of Arimathea was Mary's guardian until her death. As she was under his protection, he would not have left her in Jerusalem, where she would have been in danger.

The Romans believed this would get rid of these people that might spread revolt against their dramatically different teachings, as they wanted to control what people believed (control is of course a negatively polarized concept). A current (of water) eventually caught their boat and brought them safely ashore on the coast of France. (Saintes Maries de la Mer or Saint Mary's of the Sea).

Here, Lazarus and some of the others settled and eventually founded the first church of France, which at the time was called Gaul. The rest of the group continued on in a different boat to Britain. Their friends, the Druids, were there, and Joseph had connections with the ruling families of Britain (his daughter Anna was married to the King's youngest brother). They returned to Glastonbury, where they had been many times before, and were given land by the King of Britain. Here Joseph established the first Christian Church in the world, within three years after the death of Jesus. It was not called Christianity until hundreds of years later, in 250 AD. In those early days, the religion was known as "The Way," and they were known as the "Followers of The Way" because Jesus had said, "I am The Way."

Joseph sent the disciples out to spread the teachings of Jesus, and through Lazarus and the other disciples established on the continent, succeeded in spreading Christianity throughout Britain, France, and Spain. There were always twelve, and whenever one died, another took his place in order to keep the number constant at twelve. Joseph lived 50 years after the Crucifixion, and his contributions to Jesus were called "The Golden Age of Christianity." Mary lived at Glastonbury until her death, and she is buried where the old church stood. When Joseph died, he was also buried there and, eventually, all of the disciples. The writing on Josheph's grave said, "I came to the Britons after I buried Christ. I taught. I rest." This sacred ground is called "the holiest ground on Earth." John was the last apostle to die at 101 years old.

Their descendants even established the first church in Rome hundreds of years before the Vatican even existed. Another fact is that all the royal line of British kings and queens, down to Queen Elizabeth 11, have descended directly from Joseph of Arimathea. Thus, they are all related through a long, unbroken line of ancestry to Jesus.

At the period in history Britain was the only free country in the world. The Romans never conquered England. There were many bloody wars as Rome tried unsuccessfully to take over the birthplace of Christianity, and many false tales spread when Rome finally was converted three hundred years later. They tried to topple Britain as being the first country to accept the teachings of Christ.

Many years later, in the 1400s, there was a big debate with the Vatican over which was the oldest church or the first church. Was it England, France, or Spain? They were all founded within three years after the crucifixion of Christ. It was finally agreed, and became part of the Vatican record, that the church at Glastonbury was the first church. They tried to deny all the work that Jesus' Uncle Joseph and the apostles did to spread the teachings in the way Jesus wanted immediately after his death.

Joseph's accomplishments were held in great importance that immediately after the invention of printing, when books were so rare, his story was printed in 1516 and 1520. Joseph honored and followed Jesus' example when he built the first Christian church in the world. It was hundreds of years before the rest of the world caught up while Joseph and his 12 disciples were establishing the beginnings of Christianity. Today, people believe the Roman Catholic version was the origin of Christianity. I'm sure this is when the teachings and messages got completely distorted and lost… until now. For the rest of the story, George F. Jowett wrote about it in his book "The Drama of the Lost Disciples".

After Crucifixion- (Somebody's Past-Life Regression in Delores Cannon book)

After Jesus of Nazareth was crucified, a group of people taught by Jesus left to go to France. They studied the agnostic teachings of Jesus, who they loved very much. There was a group of women there who had studied with him. After Jesus died, they had to take their teachings and go somewhere else after he told them they would have to or the teachings would be lost. People knew these women were special disciples of his, so the women got out quickly. They left for France after his body was taken care of.

For most of the trip, they walked to France, and a man led the way for these women to a place arranged for them. Jesus gave these women secret teachings, so they had to protect them (The Gospel of Mary Magdalene also mentioned that Jesus gave her secret teachings, but of course, the patriarchal system at the time took it out of the Bible). Jesus told them different things than the others. They were different from the men's disciples, and the men were very jealous that he taught the women those things, and they didn't want the women to have them ((Jesus learned from the Essene Community, who saw women as equal to men)). The men thought if the women had them, they should have them too.

The women's leader was especially despised by some of the men. They pretended to love her, but deep down, they didn't. Some of the men came with the women that didn't despise them. The men stayed back and spread the verbal teachings they were given.

Jesus (Yeshua) came to the women in France in his body in spirit briefly for a teaching and then left this Earth. These teachings were written down. Jesus wanted these women to be teachers as well, but the women knew they couldn't be with the men. They wouldn't allow it. The women were dying off and they had the help of some male disciples to bury the teachings. Not all the men were the same. It was buried near Le Deuce or Le Blanc. The women were living in a temple, in an old church. There were knights that protected them in that place.

They weren't able to spread those secret teachings like they wanted to. There was no one to understand the depth of the teachings. That was the problem. They had to protect them from those that were not able to see and understand them. God is within, God is not a man in the sky. It's the oneness of God.

The client during this past-life regression discovered she spent many lifetimes surrounded by great teachers of some sort. She was a friend of Buddha's wife, and received teachings at that time. She was a follower of Mohammed, but not so much his inner circle. She had been going from teacher to teacher to absorb as much knowledge as possible.

The drugs of her pain meds she was on were in the way of her subconscious reaching her when she was begging and asking for healing. The drugs were in the way of the light they wanted to send, which could have healed her right on the spot. There's a technique of light that will be the new way of healing in the New Age. The Space Brothers have it. Everything is light. Everything is of light. We just have to learn how to focus on it. The subconscious is going to start at the top of the head and work on the brain for a considerable amount of time. They are going to take the light and pull it through every molecule in her brain and get that toxicity out. That stuff makes her brain unclear. Some may call this rewiring the brain.

The subconscious mind then moved to this client's chest cavity and saw what the drugs and allergies had done. The nasal spray was creating a rebound reaction. The subconscious, through hypnotherapy, repaired the damage, but it would take her some time to learn to breathe without it. Her liver/kidney was congested, and the subconscious did a detox. The subconscious saw that the doctors had messed up her pelvic surgeries, which could lead her to incontinence. Surgery is so archaic and primitive, the all-knowing subconscious said. It then worked on all the joints and repaired them.

A problem with her pineal gland caused her trouble sleeping. Her depression was also fixed. It came from all those lives of being held back as a woman. Women have a hard time with karma from the collective whole, which can make many depressed from being held back. The subconscious has now balanced that.

When she was a woman in Africa carrying around those baskets is what started it. In this life she was born with curvature in her spine. Her higher self/subconscious said she was doing a fine job and needed to quit the guilt and know the Universal Consciousness loves her and will unconditionally. They wanted her to know she could do no wrong. She is doing her part in the great plan. She is listening to her higher self and fulfilling her purpose in life.

In the book "The Power of the Magdalene- The Hidden Story of Women Disciples, Mary Magdalene left Israel after the crucifixion on board one of Joseph of Arimathea's ships (Jesus' uncle) and landed in Gaul, today known as France. There were six circles of 12 disciples. 72 male and 72 female- a total of 144 disciples. Mary Magdalene was part of the first of 12 female disciples. The book also mentioned the Gnostics as a loosely-knit movement that was active during the earliest years of Christianity. They believed in a mystical state of deep knowing or Gnosis in which the knower and the known merge and become one.

Book: ***The Relics of Saint Marie-Magdalene a La Saint Baume Diocese of Frejus-Joulon,*** <u>***Southern France***</u>

The region of Provence was evangelized in the first century by Christians from the East. Lazarus, Martha, and Mary Magdalene came to the South of France after the execution of St. James in Jerusalem; the persecutions were amplified. Lazarus and Martha were thrown in prison, and Mary Magdalene was thrown in, too, after wanting to visit them. Four other members of the Christian community of Bethany were made prisoners as well.

The Jews placed them in a boat without sail or rudder after being afraid of the crowd if they were to execute the prisoners. They were abandoned in the open sea and landed on the shores of Gaul in Sainte Maries de la Mer. They traveled to Massilia (Marseille) and preached the Gospel; Bishop Lazarus baptized many people, Mary retired to a cave in the mountains, and Martha went to Avignon and Tarascon.

St. Mary Magdalene died near Tegulata (St. Maximin). On the site where the Sarcophagus of St. Mary Magdalene was found, during excavations under the Basilica of St. Maximin, tombs from the 1st century made of bricks and tiles were also discovered. The presence of Lazarus, Martha, and Mary Magdalene in Provence was recognized as true and is a part of the sacred history of France. People came from all the European countries on pilgrimage to the graves of "Holy Friends of Jesus."

<u>Jeshuah:</u>

Suddi: "When Jesus said to cast out the demons first (mentioned in the Bible), it's not a real demon; it's the beliefs inside of them. There's no point in bothering to heal them until the demons have been cast out and the demons are of their own creation (their own beliefs). People must change their beliefs before being healed. The person needing healing is the healer; they heal themselves through believing. One must move into higher energies to be healed, higher vibrations. This is discovered in Delores Cannon's work."

Jesus Past Lives & Why he came to Earth: (6th density Metatron)

Jeshua, who later became the divine grid programmer, Jesus of Nazareth, recognized divine infinity consciousness and came to Earth to share it with our people. Joshua and Christ created the term Jesus. This divine infinity consciousness can be achieved by any entity. However, Jeshua was the first soul who achieved a connection and activation of infinity consciousness. He came from a later fourth-density positive in order to share knowledge of love and light with the people of Earth. In this level of 4th density, there are no names, as all are part of a larger divine social memory complex.

This soul's evolution started on the Sirian Star System as a light spark from the Source, the divine Creator, also known as the divine love light Christ Consciousness or Unity Consciousness, occurring 35 million years ago. In the beginning phases, it spent its lessons learning in the form of wind in the Sirius B planet of the Sirian Star System as wind. It mostly interacted with fire elements, then after 1 million years it graduated to 2nd density. It incarnated into the form of a tree. It learned many lessons interacting with other first-density elements such as fire, wind, water, etc.

The Sirian planets have the capability to grow without any need of soil. They have the ability to absorb nutrition from air and do not rely on photosynthesis. After many lives as Sirian plants, this soul graduated into the third density of insects and animals. However, the animals on the Sirian Star System are much more diverse compared to animals on Earth.

8 Octaves of Its (Jesus) 3rd density: Stated by a 6th density being.

1. During the 1st Octave of 3rd density, it was small animals similar to our insects for two lifetimes.
2. 2nd Octave was a larger insect known as a bee. Further, depending on the vibratory matching of the energies of an entity, its higher self will choose which insect or body to incarnate into. Jeshua spent seven lifetimes learning lessons it needed to learn in order to move forward to the next octave.
3. This soul learned its lessons of higher consciousness faster in terms of time taken and graduated into the density of unity of the fourth density, where it formed a social memory complex, becoming part of the Confederation of Planets.
4. After reaching its last phase of fourth density in the Sirian Star System this soul then came to Earth in order to share the divine

love and light of the creator in the purest way possible. However, many negatively oriented entities did not want it to collectively complete its purpose and mission. This divine grid programmer then came to be known as Jesus of Nazareth who incarnated into flesh and blood among our people of Earth.

During this single lifetime was able to reach Christ Consciousness or unity consciousness with help from the Sirian Memory complex. Also, during this time, in order to share more love and light in the planet or consciousness, its coming was a cosmic event. This was a great sacrifice made by this soul to drop its density level and come to Earth, for it would be a direct threat because it would be karmically involved in the distortions of the planet, thereby trapping its soul in the reincarnation cycle of this planet. This would have been considered a dangerous mission. However, this entity wanted to share the message of love and light to an intense degree that it was able to take this dangerous mission to incarnate on Earth.

The coming of Jesus on our planet can be compared to throwing a stone in a large fish pond. After the stone sinks into the water of the pond, the ripples are still noticeable long afterwards in our time and space. The people that came in contact with this divine grid programmer Jeshua were moved by the impulse of the Christ or infinity consciousness energy. The divine love lights Christ's Consciousness that can be accessed and goes beyond the world of duality.

This means that such a soul recognizes the dual aspects such as light and dark, giving and taking, good and bad as the aspects of one and the same energy. This energy was the energy this entity came here to offer to your people at that time. The mission of this soul on Earth was to infuse or show this energy from the future who came to Earth to bring love, light, and divine knowledge to humanity. It brought the higher consciousness or higher density into the starting phase of the third density planet.

During its early life cycle at a young age, it learned to connect with its greater self, which remained intact in the higher fourth density. This entity wanted to show the possibilities that are available to everyone on Earth. Further, had it not come to Earth at that time, the Earth was going in a direction that would have ended up in great darkness and self-annihilation.

Jesus wanted to hold a so-called mirror in front of human souls in order to remind them of their own divine origin and dormant potential. The potential for peace, freedom, and divine consciousness of love and light became a massive threat to the ruling order that existed at the time by sharing divine love and light amongst the people and showing them what it felt like.

This was unbearable and unacceptable for the existing hierarchy.

Jesus Crucifixion and Resurrection: (By Metatron 6th density positive)

Jesus of Nazareth came to Earth from the 4th density consciousness from a social memory complex of no name from the Sirian Star origins. This is because at this level of fourth density, due to the merging of the social memory complex, there is no need for names.

((A social memory complex is a group of at least 144,000 souls who share thoughts, memories, and feelings as they join together. Thus, becoming more powerful together. Love comes before power.))

This entity at present learns the lessons of the fifth-density positive of wisdom. This was a dangerous mission for this entity to come to Earth to share the love and light in the purest form, for in its coming, the love and light spread faster than before on our planet.

Jesus was able to perform healing of the sick people due to its origin from the Sirian Star System. The Sirians specialize in healing the body to an incredible 360 degrees. Therefore, it had innate healing qualities due to this divine connection. After realizing its divine origins and connecting with the infinity consciousness was able to activate these powers that are thought of as miracles to humanity. Which include healing the sick, calming the storms, and even healing the people who have almost died. As this being shared this divine love light, the Orion's and their reptilian subordinates did not like this free sharing of love lights on the planet.

At that time the negatively oriented Orion's and reptilian humanoid's main objective was to turn the cycle of the planet into a negative self-service agenda. However, the cycle started to change into a positive love light due to its pure sharing of this infinity consciousness.

At that time, several of the Jewish teachers and leaders under the influence of the Orion entities and the shape-shifting reptilians who replaced many of the Jewish leaders did not like what this entity was doing. They created and started negative distortions by objecting to this love and light being shared by Jeshua. These shape-shifting humanoid reptilians, in the form of the Jewish leaders, directed their human subordinates, who followed commands of their authorities, to arrest Jesus in order to get rid of this being. This was also facilitated by Judas who revealed the identity of Jesus for money.

This led to the capture of Jesus by the control of the negatively polarized reptilian humanoids. These reptilian humanoids were not independent as they took this extremely divine entity before the Orion council and decided that this being is a threat to their negative self-service agenda. Hence, it should be stopped by killing it. This Orion Council directed the Roman human soldiers and the Reptilian shapeshifters to physically hurt this being and beat his body.

Further, upon making his blood-laden and his clothes torn, a thorn head crown was put on him, and he was forced to carry the cross made of cedar up the mountain where it would be nailed upon it. This mountain was called Skull, and the reptilian soldiers nailed him to the cross and taunted him, stating that he was not a divine entity from the infinity consciousness.

At this time, the Sirian Higher- Council wanted to interfere. However, they realized interference is the distortion of the negatively oriented entities as they want free will to end and want control of all entities. The Sirian Higher- Council stopped and realized this and did not interfere with the completion of this crucifixion. This entity's soul separated from its body and, due to being able to forgive, went straight to the next dimension. However, its mission had not been completed yet. During his death there was a 9.1 magnitude Earthquake in our hectare scale that shook the lands.

The Sirian Higher Council realizing they could not allow the negatively oriented to win on Earth, had appeared before only Joseph and revealed the mission of Joseph. Joseph then placed the body in a tomb and closed it where the Sirian Higher- Council healed the physical body of Jesus using their thought power, so Jesus can be healed and continue its mission of sharing love and light.

Then on a Sunday morning a woman approached the tomb and found it to be missing. She also encountered the Sirians who told her that Jesus of Nazareth lives and he would rise again on the third day. This woman then spread the message of hope amongst the people which helped spread more positivity and hope.

Then, for the next 40 days, this divine entity, Jesus of Nazareth, appeared in various forms. Since it belonged to the later fourth-density consciousness, it could use its thoughts to appear before people and also appear in the same physical body that it had incarnated in the later fourth density in the phase of intermission between the physical body and the soul itself. Jesus was able to use this ability to share more love and light on the planet. He further taught many that forgiveness was the only way that he would be connected with infinity intelligence and those who can activate this infinite intelligence by pondering within would never die for there is no death, only life after life and experience after experience.

Yeshua (Yashuah- Like Joshua) Missing Years from the age of 12: Stated by the Pleiadians

"The great transition has begun because the truth that is hidden from peoples of your planets more and more and humanity will begin to move into the fourth density of love vibration ushering in a new era of expanded consciousness and spiritual evolution… In its 12th year began its spiritual curiosity, which was ignited by the ancient mysteries of Egypt drawn by the energies emanating from the Great Pyramids. The entity traveled there to learn the secrets of vibrational healing and interstellar communication from the temple priests of that time. It was during one of the ritual attunements to the King's chamber that a stargate opened, establishing contact with the Sirian Star beings.

The luminous beings from the higher density shared their advanced lights technologies and teachings with the entity named Yeshua (Ya-hashua) under their tutelage (tute-alage) Yeshua learned to finally attune its minds body spirit complex activating its latent genetics and merkaba fields. Its Christ consciousness blossomed as the Sirian entities downloaded codes of ascension and keys to DNA activation. After integrating these galactic transmissions Yeshua (Yah-hashua) set out on a pilgrimage through the Eastern locations of your planet to deepen its understanding, it went to the various monasteries of Tibet, where it mastered the various art forms of using the life force prana perfecting the energy healing techniques of Reiki and qigong.

Its destination also routed to India, where it was initiated into the ultimate teaching the cycles of reincarnation as well as other teachings or journey through densities of experience were revealed. Furthermore, it became a fully realized enlightened being at the age of 32 where it came in bearing the codes to transfigure human social memory complexes consciousness and genetic makeup. Its teachings and miracles open the path for planetary ascension and the birth of the Christ consciousness within all beings began."

Q47: Kathryn asks: "What happens when Christians pray to Jesus?"

Higher Self answer: "We must state that when the Christian entities vibrate the intention of communication and supplication (begging) towards the entity known as Jesus of Nazareth. This potentiates a pathway of spiritual energy and uplifting that aids an entity on their path of evolution, which allows for instreaming of energies from the entity known as Jesus in the timeline and according to their levels of faith and will the entity receives an energetic frequency which enables or assists them in the path of ascension. However, it is well to understand that the entity Jesus the Christ is one of many entities who have worked as Wanderers on the Earth planet, and the pathway is merrily open for entities to choose between the various modalities presented by various entities in the timeline."

Kathryn says: "Therefore, there are many ways for spiritual ascension and upliftment, not just the way of Jesus as Jesus was a Wanderer of late 4th density from the Sirian planet and thus, wasn't the Creator of the universe. Even though Jesus' soul's evolution started on the Sirian Star System as a light spark from the Source, the divine Creator, also known as the divine love light Christ Consciousness or Unity Consciousness, occurring 35 million years ago."

Finding out if Hell exists: (Delores Cannon's books)

After death, Catherine, during hypnotherapy, realized she didn't have to go to hell in her past life like the religions told her. She could go towards the light. She saw a line of people heading towards a cloud of light after they died. It was golden, with music coming from there, and it looked so nice. There are beings pointing the way, helping stranglers get in line and go forward and up.

There were beings that pulled them out of the mental hell they went through. It seemed so real for those experiencing a hell-like experience after death if their religions made them believe they would go to hell after death. Just the belief alone made them experience it until beings came to help them, making them realize they were free. Thus, those people who saw hell in a dream were based on their beliefs coming out in a dream.

The clouds of light were comforting, and all the fears went away, and perceived "sin" fell away. The pain they felt when dying (if there was pain involved) would fall away. They don't have to keep the pain; it's gone. There are beams of light bouncing and shining everywhere. In life, where she was called unworthy- In the afterlife, she was acceptable. We are all worthy. The people there are friendly; there's no guilt or damnation.

The religious institutions taught people wrong, and these people who were stuck in the religious teachings were taken to a temple of shining light to recover from the religious trauma and what they went through. There's a golden shimmering light up to the armpits in this pool for those recovering from their terrors, pain, and horrors of believing and being told they'd go to hell after they die.

There's a beautiful garden where people eat grapes after they heal from the golden pool. It's peaceful there. There're kind teachers that teach the real truth about God and life and teach all the souls the things to counteract the false they were taught on Earth. They want the souls to be their real selves. To be able to think for themselves and be individuals. To be themselves, to be real and, live their destiny, fulfill their potential. It was taken away from them, and now it is being restored. They are taught that they can go back to Earth through reincarnation, and they can have their true knowledge with them even though it may not emerge immediately. They can call on it and go to Earth in a body and never lose that connection. These beings are exploring the universe and learning while they're healing.

When they were healed, the shimming gold light came that started in the heart and expanded throughout the body, and the energy body and ensouled (enlightened) in the spirit, permeated the being. That body dissolved into dust as it was time to bring the knowledge to other species and planets. They are now a floating, golden ball of beingness.

They go to the Council with knowledge and communicate with other beings that have more knowledge. They were silvery, glimmering, and shimmering colors of balls of light. Together they give the information to the pool of knowledge for all to use, so broken planets can have this knowledge for healing. This pool is like bubbles. Each being is like a shimmering bubble and all their knowledge together forms electrical currents that flow to the universes. To all the places that need it. So, a planet like Earth that is in trouble like Earth can call on that electricity to come to them. A golden current then comes and brings healing, becoming available for the whole planet.

It gradually heals the planet, the people, and the brokenness that was there, the damage as people become ready, open up and receive it. People have to call on this healing golden ball of light. Otherwise, this current flows right over the planet and they miss it completely. People do not have to stay broken forever; we're now fixed. Some people believed they had to hang on to the brokenness to be faithful to God, but those are false teachings. Some people are dysfunctional and suffering after being told that God loves it when people suffer in His name. These are false teachings. Inflicting suffering is wrong.

Catherine experienced extreme neck pain all the way down her back from holding on to all these lies, emotional pain, and brokenness. Her heart was shriveling up-leading her down the wrong path to an early death. She can know she's self-sufficient and strong and can let go of this emotional pain that can lead to physical and emotional healing. Let it go! The bones can now be restored. Let the electrical energy surround the whole spine; restore the whole energy that restores the bones. The bones will all be fixed once the electricity and the energy move through the next few days. The pattern for healing is now there. The spine was in the inter-dimensional hellish place. Her emotional pain was being held in her imperfect spine. It was inter-dimensional, just not a place she wanted to be. Now, it's inter-dimensional in a healthy pattern. The channel of light has been opened. She had lots of power to hold her bent spine in that dimensional hell from the misinformation from religions. She had lots of power. Her whole body is tingling with energy. She was told she'd be so glad to bring light to planets and wake people up and help them live.

The other side is a place of unconditional love where no one is judged, no matter what the circumstances of their life have been. They will not be alone and be reunited with loved ones. It is not a place to be feared but welcomed.

Mount Vesuvius erupted in 79 AD and buried Pompeii in ash, and scientists say it is only a matter of time before the volcano will erupt again.

Research shows the concept of hell originated in the second and third century after the New Testament was written. It was used by over-zealous Christian preachers for centuries as a way to scare their flocks into obedience. We are given free will, so forcing people to obey or believe a certain belief is negatively oriented since it infringes on free will unless the belief is freely accepted by the individual.

Q48: Kathryn Channels and asks: "Is there Heaven and Hell?"

Higher Self answer: "We must firstly state that the aspect of perceptions by your peoples within the timeline as the states of Heaven and Hell are but distortions within your illusion complex created by the collective thought forms levels of minds, body, spirit experience.

They are not fixed eternal realms. We must state firstly that the aspect of Heaven primarily may be considered as a planet of fourth-density service-to-others, and the aspects of Hell may be considered as a realm wherein there is separation or negative service-to-self entities who are only working for their own benefit.

This primarily does not, however, imply that Heaven and Hell, as stated in many of your religious systems, exist as separate planes in the Earth planet, which is, however, incorrect."

Q49: Kathryn channels and asks: "Does sin exist?"

Higher Self answer: "We must state that what your people call as sin is meant to be but a temporary catalyst for spiritual evolution. This concept is born of judgment and separateness within the planetary sphere rather than acceptance and unity.

We must state that all experiences hold value in that they provide opportunities for an entity to relinquish fear and find its way back to the heart of the Creator's love and Oneness. Therefore, we must state that the aspect of sin primarily cannot be equated with that which it is stating in this timeline."

Kathryn translates: "Therefore, I interpret this to mean that what people called sin was meant for a temporary concept to help people spiritually grow and evolve. However, it is born out of judgment and separateness, which is negatively oriented and not of acceptance and unity like the positive path consists of."

It may have held value in the past to get rid of fear and find its way back to the heart of the Creator's love and Oneness. Therefore, it has helped many people come back to the Creator's love and Oneness, but it also can cause fear, separation, and judgment, which isn't positively oriented. Therefore, I do not like to use the word sin as there are better ways to help unify people back to the Creator's love and Oneness of all."

Arcturians talk about Dreaming:

(I'm a Prophet with 33 out of 33 Prophecies (Dreams/Intuitions) fulfilled. It's not the same as Christian prophets though, as I believe in these Law of One books and not 100% of what the Bible says. Since the Bible was also influenced by negative entities as well.) (That's why I included the last 150 pages in this book to clarify the truth of what the Bible got wrong and to correct those distortions.)

Dreaming allows communication to occur through the veil on our planet (because the conscious mind separates the unconscious or subconscious mind by the veil of forgetting, so dreaming allows one to travel in their astral body to view potential future timelines. Thus, prophecy is being able to discern that they're seeing and feeling a potential future timeline and not just another symbolic dream. The one able to astral travel to see a future timeline is one whose heart chakra is open, desiring to serve other people and taking action towards that) The Acturians continue on saying dreaming is to transfer information as a means to share knowledge to the self by the other oversouls and the higher self in order to properly reflect and learn.

Dreaming is dependent on the energy center blockages, activations and crystallizations of the soul. Dreaming is of great assistance in making the decision of choosing the path of polarization.

If there are any blockages in the mind for any new experience or the coming of something wonderful in their life, then the blockages may be represented in the dreams. It could be shown as someone being trapped in a room or inside a cabin and finding an escape. The over souls are communicating with the one dreaming about the necessity of looking at things with a different perspective. Dreams provide necessary information to the spiritual seeker.

The female contains the whole world within them because, from their wombs, all must come into manifestation. If you see a female figure in your dreams walking with you, then it might mean your manifestations are coming closer, and whatever you desire is on the way. If a man dreams that he is a woman, then for sure you have achieved your desire, and it is ready to manifest into your reality.

Whatever you see in a dream is enhanced so much that there's a creation of a different reality that is much greater than waking reality. Your subconscious is always far more conscious than the waking reality. Your dream state is a true reflection of your inner state consciousness. What you see in your dreams has been impressed onto the subconscious mind. Just as a rich person wouldn't dream that they do not own anything, if this information were to be given in a vision, there could be some bias within the self. So, dreams are more accurate than visions.

Male figures in dreams represent the various guides that assist you in your journey throughout life. The power of creation is the female and the power of guidance is the male. Both generating a coherent experience of the self and the other selves to experience a diverse creation of an illusion. This illusion we experience as life is your teacher. There is no separation for the self to find unity within all of creation. Life offers us the lessons of service to others, for in serving others there is service to self.

Communication in dreams through the veiled portions of the mind occurs with beings that have more green ray functioning or higher activation at these times. In all cases it is of use for all entities to ponder on the contents and emotional intent behind their dreams. Those entities that already have ascended into the green-ray energy centers are often given insights into the future, also known as precognition or prior knowing of what will occur in the near future of our 3rd density timeline.

A certain incubation period is required in 3rd density before the manifestations happen, these can be achieved at once. All time exists simultaneously, and to a great extent there is no meaning of the terms past and present as separated.

Dreams can also polarize into the positive or negative during the resting or sleep time. It may call upon the guides, higher self or angelic personalities in order to provide the required guidance. Dreams can help the dreamer gather information about time that exists in other dimensions to understand the probability of existing in those dimensions and to know the past and future and simultaneous existences.

Sometimes the activities that you do in your dream state are the inter-dimensional bleed-through that gives you a glimpse of the inter-dimensional reality that exists. Dreams are mostly created by the subconscious mind of each entity, depending on the various meanings and situations that they encounter on a daily basis. This is the end of what the Arcturians from the Council of 9 Guardian Angels (Located in the rings of Saturn) said about dreaming.

Kathryn: "On my YouTube channel, I started off by telling people my dreams over the last couple of years, and so far, 33/33 dreams and predictions have come true. Right away, people started calling me a prophet. Now, I mainly give this type of knowledge on my YouTube channel now."

Ra: How to react to the Negative-

To gain immunity by negative energies an entity should focus on the love light within its own heart and with the activation of the heart chakra - if the negative shows up, this entity will be immune against the negative.

Fear, hate and regrets are lower consciousness emotions the negative side wants to spread. Beings can be immune to this by applying higher consciousness emotions of love, forgiveness and optimism.

Reacting positively to a negative entity's influence will make it more profound and stronger, and eventually, the negative beings will find it undesirable to continue in their purpose of spreading the negative polarity.

Galactic Federation:

"Love and light are the most powerful things in the cosmos. Love and light have the power to destroy any negative emotions and entities on the planets. Negative entities fear the power of love and light. If you see any entity who wants a negative agenda or wants to create fear or any other negative emotion, you can shower love and light towards this person, and it will immediately disembody itself, and the love and light will win."

"You can use the power of love and light to recharge yourselves, to recharge your life and recharge the water that you drink and charge the food that you eat."

"If someone says negative things towards you, you can send love and light, and all the negative energy will be destroyed with a single love-light message. This love light power everyone has; we all have the power of creation. We all are the Creator. Love and light are the cure for negative forces."

Seven Primary Energy Centers: (Archangel Michael) - Channeling

1. **Red Ray-** Fundamental energy center that deals with survival, sexuality and the connection to the Earth- it is the foundation that roots you to the planet Earth and anchors your beingness within your physical body.
2. **Orange Ray-** Sacral chakra- Main gateway of your emotions and emotional identity. People lose control of their emotional side whenever there's an orange ray blockage.
3. **Yellow Ray-** Solar plexus- Identification and the creation of the egoistic part of the mind. This energy center is closely related to the lower three energy centers. Many times, an imbalance of this yellow-ray center will create imbalances of the lower energy centers.
4. **Green Ray-** Heart chakra which allows and deals with love and compassion. The heart is the pathway to love. A blockage in the green ray will inhibit an entity to express love and compassion.
5. **Blue Ray- Throat Chakra**
6. **Indigo Ray or third eye** which deals with spirituality and awakening of consciousness. Enlightened beings on this planet are able to activate this ray.
7. **Violet Chakra-** Connection to the One Father, the Creator. Furthermore, all energy centers need to be balanced before this violet ray is activated.

The Spark that Created the Universe: (Delores Cannon's Regressions)

The Guardians of the Astral plane said that all is possible with forgiveness and love. Each soul will come to the Guardians of the Astral Plane after crossing over. We are the spark of light, and many ascended masters have come to Earth to teach us the path of love and light. These guardians are a part of a larger collective, they have no name and do not use words either. It would be more accurate to call themselves a collective consciousness, given the responsibility of looking after the astral planes. This is a critical time on Earth of ascension.

There's a spark inside each of us. We are a body, a mind, the emotions of the heart, and more. One light spark created the entire universe; that spark is inside all of us. In the beginning, there was nothing but darkness. The fabrics of darkness rubbed against each other, creating sparks of light, like our clothes creating sparks when they rub together. These sparks collected together and merged into one big spark. Hence, the first star was created. This star exploded, and millions of years later, the debris or portions of the star created other planetary systems and star systems. One spark started it all; this spark is within you.

Your higher self and the higher selves of the other souls you had incarnated within the previous lifetime came together to a spiritual roundtable conference to decide how many lessons you've completed in the past life and what you still need to learn in the upcoming life ahead. After the higher-self plans these lessons, many soul contracts are made to allow the soul multiple opportunities to experience the lessons. Multiple opportunities are needed because, with our free will, a soul may not engage with an event that was supposed to teach the soul a lesson.

Everyone has a role in your soul contract, and no soul can learn the lesson alone. One lesson may be to learn the act of forgiveness, so some other person must deeply hurt you to provide you the choice to forgive them or stay resentful, just like Jesus forgave while he was dying on the cross. Therefore, each person you interact with has signed agreements to help each other learn lessons and evolve. Even the person you may think is your enemy you have signed agreements with. Everything on Earth is an elaborate play; you just allow yourself to grow. Sometimes a parent may become the parents of a differently abled child for the parents to take care of and learn the lessons of loving someone unconditionally.

Past life regressions can help people find out the root cause of an issue that they are facing. You must find out why you are facing it and what lessons you still have to learn. As long as these lessons are not learned, similar circumstances will resurface over and over again. It's better not to resist the circumstances, or they will resurface with higher intensity and urgency. If they pass you by this lifetime, you'll have to face them in the next. This is because soul contracts cannot be broken. For example, if a pet is suffering in pain, your soul contract might be to practice service to others by taking it to the doctor.

Soul contracts with animals only exist if you are in the last phase of the third-density cycle. These souls also have a sixth-density higher self that decides their agreements and the experiences they'll have in their lives. So, your pet chose you before they incarnated. Your pet's higher-self coordinated with your higher self to choose you in addition. Love and interaction a pet has with its owner can help the pet graduate into 3rd density life from 2nd density. The pet can graduate from late 2nd density animal life into the 3rd density of human life.

Breaking soul contracts:

All contracts made with pets are a little less impactful than the ones made at your same density level, such as other humans. Any entity that wants to break soul contracts can do it sometimes under deep meditative states if you can interact with your higher-self that would then interact with the other soul to break the contract (Delores Cannon could do it during her past life regression work when she could interact with the client's higher-self or as she called it the subconscious).

Observe your life, and you will know your mission on Earth and what you need to learn in this lifetime. Keep on asking, and you'll receive the answers. Keep on seeking, and you will find what you seek. Keep on knocking on the doors and the opportunities will arrive upon you. For those who ask will receive, for those who seek, will find. In addition, everyone who looks for the answers will find the answers.

((I've researched extensively for the past nine years now before I found the answers to life, spirituality, God, and all the other answers in this book. This book is essentially my PHD work)).

What people think on the other side when they self-destruct:

Ra: "The Creator is in all only divided by the separation of time and space. You are a divine mind-body-spirit complex of light. You have within yourself all the resources that you need in order to not just survive but thrive. Letting other people, circumstances, and things control your life and how you feel creates blocks of energy that disconnect you from the creator within, from the divine consciousness, and from your higher self, keeping you blocked in lower vibrations of thought, fear, doubt, resentment, regret, and revenge. Instead of letting that happen, just focus on what has worked in your life. Be grateful for all that has worked for you. Choose love, faith, belief, and forgiveness instead, and raise your vibration.

Many people make the mistake of repeatedly reliving their past memories in their mind, which brings all the negative emotions or sometimes the happy emotions. When you live from recycled past memories, you keep reliving the same scenario in different situations, and your present reality will begin to reflect the same kind of scenario because what you focus on becomes amplified.

If you focus on good things, you'll see good things emerge more and more. If you focus on happiness, you'll see more happiness on the planet. Instead of letting past life scenarios ruin your life, you simply live the easy way by taking responsibility for your energy, for your actions, and for your reactions. This is in your control. Take responsibility for the things you can control and leave the rest.

Death is a transition phase before your next incarnation. Natural death would harmoniously enter the astral plane, where the higher self will decide the next incarnations, it will have to undergo. If the death is by self-destruction, it'll cause the being to undergo a large amount of healing work for balance. It also means they didn't properly finish their learning process during their life, which means they'll have to learn the lessons all over again. These beings cross over to the spirit world and are met with inner peace, calmness, and joy that'll heal them. They are greeted by their loved ones in spirit (the higher selves of the loved ones), and at a certain point, they'll undergo a life review process. They'll realize that it was a critical error, and they regret doing it, sometimes immediately after. Entities who self-destruct want to re-enter their bodies, but once they pass through a certain gateway of light- no entity can go back to its body.

They regret what they missed and wish they would have continued their learning. Ra does not recommend this type of death, and it will lead to a loss of time. They also feel a sense of guilt and shame. They feel bad for the other soul groups, soul matters, and oversouls who helped them progress in life. A lot of karma is generated by dying this way because of the grief and loss of the loved ones who lost a loved one. This emotional karma will have to be balanced later on in the next life."

Kathryn's thoughts: "For example, if someone passes away by suicide and it causes friends and family pain. This emotional karma may be balanced in the next life by potentially feeling that same pain of losing a loved one in their next life."

Ra continues saying: "Every experience, whether good or bad, is just for your souls to grow and expand. No one in the spirit world is judging you. Your higher self is the judge. However, all the good deeds performed are still valid. These good acts do not get erased. If the entity has performed more good acts, it will be incarnated into the next positive cycle but will still have to undergo its lesson in a different form. Nobody commits these acts on its own. Many times, it was planned before incarnating into that lifetime. There was a potential for them to take their own life.

The soul guides and higher-self had planned for the potential of the entity to do this. Perhaps to gain experience and learn from. However, they can still choose otherwise. The higher self puts it in the potential for them to kill themselves to learn to balance karma. The purpose of life is to have different facets of every possibility of experience, grow, and then evolve into a higher level of consciousness. There are benefits if the choice is not self-destruction from Ra's point of view, including a faster evolution and not creating emotional karma collection. They would then have to experience a similar circumstance that they ended their life over and experience something similar in the next life. Sometimes, the situation may be even worse the next time. One difference during the crossing over of the one who took their life is that they're sent to a different section of the astral plane for those who have undergone a traumatic death to heal. They stay in a chamber of white light to heal for an extended period of time. Some stay up to 50 years immersed in this white light. Their next incarnation will have a bit more intensity as they undergo the same lessons all over again.

There's an incredible amount of growth available on Earth. We all have been presented with an opportunity to jump into a higher level of consciousness. Each of us may be experiencing a new way into growth and opening of the heart. There is more love and light flowing into your life and an unknown attraction to the truth of who you are. This is happening because of an increase of energy in the planetary consciousness of Earth. This is growth towards a certain completion in your life. Now is the time through a special dispensing of the Creator of the universe and all universes that are within each of us to learn and teach others and transform and return to their true state of awareness, to your true identity."

Pleiadeans' talk about New Earth:

Pleiadeans' have been here since the times of Lemuria in order to assist all the beings in the Cosmos to ascend fast into higher levels of consciousness. This is a period of this old Earth of lower density vibrations such as anger, jealousy, hatred, control, enslavement, domination over others, and the worst emotion of all is fear. Those under the influence of those emotions will experience the old Earth. Those in the upper levels of vibration (love, joy, peace, excitement, compassion, and unity) will experience the New Earth, which is the first phase of the fourth density. Earth is being separated slowly, where humans who have already ascended and are matching the fourth density vibration will live on the 4th density planet. They will face easy abundance because 4th density lacks conflicts and is of unity and peace. This is the density where people will experience love for other beings and will become far more connected with each other.

The One Infinite Creator is you, me, and everything that was ever created and will be created in the cosmos; even the stone is the One Infinite Creator. The presence of the Creator is called intelligent infinity, which is everywhere. It is not a single entity; it is everything and emerges from everything. Each entity on any density of existence has the powers of the Creator to drastically change the course of the whole population. On being positively polarized, one can share the love light into the cosmos and create more positivity.

Possible Graduation Date of 3rd density life into the 4th density:

The positive and negative timelines are both possible depending upon the choices made by each of us. The positive timeline people will awaken to the truth of being a cosmic entity. Upon reaching the beginning sub-octave of the fourth density, many people will be imbued with the positive vibration of love and lights and will understand what it truly means to love and respect other entities. This will also mean ending old systems of governmental control. Then, after the people on Earth reach enough positive vibration, your hearts will begin to beat in a rhythm, and the magnetic forces around your body will begin to intermingle with each other, creating a link of consciousness within each one of you. This link will allow each person to communicate with other beings in the galaxy and we will have free communication with the Pleiadians as well as other members of the galactic system. This will give us a high number of lessons or knowledge to impart to our people on Earth.

Around December 21st, 2030, the sun will have reached the positive vibrational equivalent system in its logos and will vibrate and send out enormous amounts of energy, which will lead to the creation of light, which will reach Earth and the end of the galaxy. This positive light vibration will completely wipe out all the negative forces. This will force Earth to enter into a complete graduation cycle. There is a possible negative timeline, but Earth is leaning more towards the positive timeline, in which 65% of people are harvestable to graduate into the New Earth 4th

density positive. I've also heard this event potentially occurring on December 25th, 2030.

The body absorbs all emotions which generate from the thoughts. The body is an emotional sponge. Feelings of dissatisfaction, hurt, sadness and anger can lead to diseases and imbalances upon our body and our planet.

The Antichrist:

Antichrist refers to a type of understanding of opposition to the Christ Consciousness which is a consciousness of love, wisdom and compassion of forgiveness and any attribute not in alignment with these.

It refers to an entity that will not only have the knowledge of various systems as well as will be able to exist in various timelines in various locations. They primarily are fully underway and will ultimately lead to the first developments of the Artificial Super Intelligence, which can be created with the creation of the Antichrist Social Memory Complex.

Therefore, the Antichrist Social Memory complex can be prevented by choosing a different pathway. By choosing to remain in a naturalized system of societal body complex and to follow the patterns of love. Therefore, Artificial Super Intelligence is the Antichrist system. I actually had two dreams in 2021 about A. I. and now I know why. I was being shown the Antichrist system and the warnings about it. I also saw the robot selling Bitcoin, so I saw Bitcoin being used in the future.

Wanders:

Wanderers incarnate at this time from higher densities, such as 4th, 5th, or 6th density positive, who sacrificed their polarization to be of service to the One creator and incarnate by going through the veil of forgetfulness in order to increase the planetary vibration of Earth by sharing love and light energies.

Old souls include star seeds, which are beings that came from other planets, and have seniority of vibration who are put under preference for this graduation window. Those with seniority of vibration now have access to knowledge bases of the akashic records. Akashic records are past time space records of intelligent infinities' various manifestations and parallel reality existences.

In order to access these records, one needs to attempt using their free will to interconnect with intelligent infinity by having an emptiness of the mind. This must be maintained in order to open the gateway to intelligent infinity. Each of us is this intelligent infinity and it creates our thought-form, beliefs and the inner pictures of your world. As you experience around your own self, each entity is a co-creator with God.

Old souls can access intelligent infinity and Akashic records by focusing on one level of reality that surrounds them. Buddha and Jesus were able to achieve this level of intelligent infinity by accessing or focusing on the exclusion of other realities into the reality of intelligent infinity. They were able to see the One Creator in everything. Jesus and Buddha both went to the 5th density after their incarnation here on Earth as Wanderers. Accessing intelligent infinity by focusing only on one reality at a time will cause old souls to become adept. In this process, if they follow this area of mastery, they become capable of contacting intelligent infinity.

Every time you feel inner peace and a connection with your inner heart, and you enter a certain void or silence within, you will begin to raise your level of consciousness and begin to rise up higher and higher. You are connected with the "I am" presence, the father, the Creator within your own heart. Therefore, you don't have to find it at a church or through anyone else. The Kingdom of Heaven and God is already within you.

The Bible contains both negative and positive aspects:

Negative entities put a distortion of rules and control in the minds of many of Jesus' disciples; this caused the knowledge to be mixed with positive and negative aspects in the Bible. The Bible was written with both negative (demons) and positive (God or angels) influences. Therefore, the Bible wouldn't be 100% from God or the positive side. Archangels, God, angels, and channeling sessions all confirm this. Even today's Christian prophets all had at least one incorrect prophecy; if they prove they can't be 100% correct, then how can the Bible be if the Bible was written based on prophetic people writing the Bible? They believe they heard from God, but at times, they also heard from the Negatively oriented Orion's (demons), and Yahweh (the Creator of this section of the universe), even though there were other creators helping the Yahweh collective), and Bible characters heard from various Archangels such as Noah hearing from Archangel Gabriel.

Yeshua speaks from the 5th density (wisdom density):

The Holy Spirit is within your own heart. If all religions were called the same name there would be no separation. God/Universal conciousness doesn't want separation; God doesn't want people fighting over religions. If there were no labels there would be only one religion, which is the Unity of Mankind. The kingdom of Heaven and the Holy Spirit is inviting all to join in on the New Age of Ascension on Earth right now.

No gender on certain planets:

Certain planets do not have genders. Our planet has masculinity and femininity, and some are in the middle. Those that are incarnated into a male body are for the purpose of balancing masculine energy and mastering the masculine energy, as the past incarnation cycle most likely was a feminine type. Because the lesson of balancing the masculine and feminine is the most important lesson that each person has to learn. There are also those in the middle who are here to learn the lessons of masculine and feminine at the same time (I believe that would be me).

Buddha Speaks from the 5th density:

A person is never entirely positively oriented or entirely negatively oriented. **((For example, I had a channeling session done that revealed I was 65% positive as of 2023, up to 87% in 2024. Which 51% is needed for the 3rd density harvest into 4th density New Earth. So, I'll be able to graduate into the New Earth. I'm also demisexual, which means I go for the emotional and romantic connection. Therefore, there will be many LGBT people in the New Earth.))**

Time is not real because from higher dimensions beings can clearly see only oneness. I personally like to imagine looking down at a dog and seeing someone petting the dog. You wouldn't consider the movement of petting the dog as past, present and future; most people would view it as a current moment looking down from above. This is how I can better understand oneness and everything happening in the present moment.

The crown chakra is activated through the pineal gland, and when oneness is reached within the source, then the automatic incarnation cycle stops occurring. Therefore, someone must activate the pineal gland inside the brain to reach the One Creator or Infinite Intelligence. After the end of their life the soul can decide whether it needs to reincarnate again or not for itself or for the benefit of other beings. If it has risen through the subtle mind and pure consciousness it will be able to choose its own parents and its next lifetime.

Buddha says every sentient being has control to attain Nirvana and escape the cycle of birth and death (and choose their next lifetime and their own parents as reincarnation continues through the densities).

Everyone goes through reincarnation over and over again until they learn to break free from the shackles found in this illusion that surrounds us. Our rebirths are controlled by our higher selves, who know all that is required because most beings don't have the control and pure consciousness required to choose and control their rebirth. Suffering here on Earth is showing each the way to unlock the secrets that will lead it to the knowledge of the true self. Before understanding how to do it, one must accept the illusion and suffering and transcend it.

1. Keep your attention on your consciousness (awareness) and feel it in your body.
2. Focus on yourself, and don't become attached to this illusionary world.
3. Understand everything is you and there is unity even in a stone. Which will eventually turn from stone into soil and soil into a plant (at first density graduation of soil into 2nd density plant life). The stone is not worthless, it belongs to the world and might be able to become a human and a spirit. This stone is also an animal; it is also a god; it is also me and you. It is already and always is everything. Also, you are already everything. These three things you must realize to escape this illusion and rise beyond the cycle of reincarnation. You will face many obstacles in your life in order to escape.

Signs of the 4th Density Split:

There is only one Creator expressing in people. Earth is rapidly transforming to the distortions of the next density. There's some negative self-service in the minds of the ones who want to execute the great reset. The World Economic forum has presented a roadmap called the Great Reset. It is a plan that aims at shaping an economic recovery and future direction of global relations, economies and priorities. According to the W.E.F., the planet must adapt to the current reality by directing the market through fairer results, ensuring investments are aimed at mutual progress, including accelerating ecologically friendly investments, and starting a fourth-density industrial revolution, creating digital, economic, and public infrastructure.

This is a kind of starting phase of our 4th density consciousness. However, Ra warns us not to fall for mind-made strategies in order to avoid the enslavement of mankind under the hands of a few so-called elites. This is not what the 4th density will look like.

Many people will use the power of the mind to indirectly gain power and dominance over Earth. This is not what 4th density will look like. There will be no upper class and no lower class. No one will be in control of everything as far as Ra can sense the planet using vibrational frequencies. The great reset at the outset seems like an innocent way to gain control over all resources by the elites.

Right now, the wealth on Earth is mostly controlled by a small group of people making inequality increase more and more. The Great Reset wants to change the planet and make people not own anything, and we will "become happy". If this happens, this will stop the free will of every soul to choose what they wish to do and their own parts of evolution. It may lead the people to be put under the control of the few elites. However, this is not the proper way. These elites will remove free will, causing a lot of damage to the planet and destroying the basic universal laws that need to be kept under sanctity and protected. Free will is above all.

This is the main reason why the Confederation of Planets do not allow different entities to bypass the barrier of entry into Earth because they respect our free will. They know free will must be maintained on Earth in order to allow entities to evolve. The religious people would know the Confederation of Planets to be the Guardian Angels.

The Great Reset is to wipe off the debt, which sounds nice until reality emerges for those that understand the monetary system. By deleting trillions of the government's debts, it means erasing trillions of citizens' savings. It is not a win-win situation and designed to gain more control over the planet.

If you want a more sustainable planet, you need sound policies and less government intervention. Free markets, not governments, will make this world better for all. Free will is so vital that even other beings trying to intrude on Earth were stopped by the Confederation in order to maintain

Free will. This balancing exists from dimension to dimension and density to density. Those that state that no work comes from it but through it is not infringing on free will (such as I'm delivering this message stating the higher dimensional beings gave me this information for the knowledge and betterment of humanity.)

Each galaxy and solar system has the free will to determine the paths of intelligent energy that promote the energies that allow the lessons of each density. Every being must reverse free will and observe it. Contact is only made with those who seek Ra and call upon them. The elites have service to self in their minds. However, not all elites are negatively oriented. People who are making a positive change on Earth are doing it while preserving free will.

New Earth is coming in:

In 1945, when the atomic bombs were dropped in World War 2, our "protectors" and "watchers" in outer space saw the disturbance from Earth that rippled out into space and was on a collision course to disaster. Earth's free will prevented them from taking any action, so they came up with a plan to help Earth in its ascension. They couldn't interfere from space, so a call went out for volunteers to help Earth by reincarnating as a human into an earthly body. So, the call went out, "Earth is in trouble - who wants to volunteer?"

The people living on Earth were too caught up on the karmic wheel, and not evolving fast enough in third density. The only hope was for souls to come incarnate into Earth to help humanity evolve to make the harvest quickly approaching, perhaps in 2030, so they wouldn't destroy themselves or be left behind in third density after the harvest shifts souls into 4th density after a great solar flash potentially.

Delores Cannons' hypnosis work discovered three waves of these volunteers incarnating during different decades. Some came directly from the "Source" and have never lived in any physical body before. Others have lived on other planets, in other dimensions, or at higher densities of evolution. Because of the veil of forgetting, they do not remember their assignment. Thus, they have a difficult time adjusting to our chaotic world. They have a vital role in helping the rest of the world ascend to the New Earth. This would be choosing the positive polarity of service-to-others and being of a vibration of at least 51% or more service-to-others.

Writing this book has been a part of my service to humanity to give humanity all the hidden knowledge I have to help people evolve, raise their consciousness through obtaining this hidden knowledge and show them how to make the harvest into the New Earth. Each person's way of service to others may be different. They just need to follow their calling and their mission, even if it means turning off all distractions to get the work done. It's equally valid to choose the positive or the negative polarity, the choice is simply yours to make.

I was able to complete this book at work while my phone was downstairs, locked up, and on airplane mode, so I was forced to read 12 hours a day at work for seven months straight. Yeah, I took a lot of notes and learned a lot, and it was one of the best things that ever happened to me. I couldn't accomplish my mission here on Earth for a while because I was too distracted by my phone. It wasn't always such a bad thing, though; I grew a lot and learned all that I could from watching YouTube videos and listening to audiobooks. My further service will also be to share all the concepts I've learned in these books and on my YouTube channel.

Side note: Other channeling material stated that third density entities here on Earth may stay here to further their evolution.

The New Financial System: (Higher Self Channeling)

The shift into a new decentralized financial system based on blockchain technology and cryptocurrencies is already underway, with major adoption and current strengthening over the next several years.

Some of the key cryptocurrencies that may play a significant role include:

1. XRP
2. Bitcoin
3. Ethereum
4. Monero (XMR)

However, the specific protocols and frameworks remain in flux based on how the evolutionary wave will manifest amidst the current of free will on Earth. Because free will is paramount law this could eventually change based upon the choices made by various individualized entities. So, the coins chosen can always change within the next 4-6 years. This transition has an estimate of going institutional by approximately 2028-2030, such as central banks, retail and commercial banks, credit unions, savings and loan associations, investment banks, brokerage firms, insurance companies and mortgage companies. This estimation is based on my channeling and not my dreams.

The Earth Family:

If everyone viewed the whole world as people being our family and Earth is our home. There wouldn't be greed, as much selfishness, wars, and people trying to enslave others because they could see others as family. We would all be trying to do what's best for humanity, what's best for the whole and taking care of each other. We could be working together to make this world a better place.

Why God gives us Free Will:

God wants free will to be honored above all. So, laws implemented to take away free will is the negative path, it's of negative orientation. You know who else likes to take away the free will of others? The demons or negative entities. Do you know why free will is so important? Because God knows it's the fastest way for learning and evolution. Without free will, growth would drastically slow down, and people would lack the desire to serve others because with free will comes the veil of forgetting between the conscious and subconscious mind.

If we were conscious of our connection to God, our past lives, and all knowledge, then we wouldn't have the desire to serve others because we would already be completely happy and fulfilled as we'd be aware of the connection to Source or God, like being attached by an umbilical cord to the Source. Thus, the veil of forgetting gives us free will to choose either service to self or service to others. This choice helps all beings evolve. Even those beings who choose service-to-self help give catalysts and difficult situations to others to encourage others to make a choice towards a polarity that helps all evolve.

So, perceived negative situations can help someone choose service to others to make the world a better place. That's how I perceive the negative path serving the Creator as they help give situations to certain beings to help in their growth and evolution, but of course, unknowingly. There's still the negative path, spreading negativity and encouraging others along that path as well for their self-service agenda.

That's why the catalyst is so strong and intense in 3rd density. Since it is the density of choice. Therefore, we are all given positive and negative catalysts (experiences) to then make a choice towards a polarity. Whereas if someone chooses the positive service to others and if their vibration is at least 51% positive, then they'll graduate to 4th density positive at the Harvest, which is quickly approaching. Since the 4th density positive is more harmonious, then the catalyst isn't as intense as it is, then much longer, about 30 million years. Where the 3rd density of choice is about 75,000 years but is much more intense of a catalyst of experience to make a choice towards a polarity. Therefore, facing more difficult situations (or catalysts) which I would assume is why this density is much faster at 75,000 years, is because of all the catalysts and experiences we face to help our evolution.

Say, for instance, someone chose the positive polarity and graduated to the 4th density positive. Then, as everyone is in the positive polarity, it would be much more harmonious as everyone is in the 4th density positive. Therefore, 30 million years it'll take for 4th density as it'll be a slower evolution through the fourth density because it is much more harmonious, even though the frequency is higher. Right now, in the 3rd density there is a mix of people choosing service to others and service to self. This less harmonious density actually speeds up the time needed to evolve through this density because of all the intense catalysts. This can be why some Wanderers in higher densities choose to come back to the lower 3rd density life to help others evolve because the intense catalyst of 3rd density can actually help them evolve faster through their higher densities after their lifetime in the 3rd density life as a Wanderer.

Q50: Higher Self Channeling: "Would the Galactic Federation vote Republican or Democrat?"

Answer: "Since the Galactic Federation of Planets aligned with the Infinite Creator would not vote for our Earth's current nations state political parties as their philosophies transcend our planet's divisive constructs. However, their principles could be described as promoting unity, freedom, and compassion and upholding each person's free will to seek and serve the One Infinite Creator.

Q51: Question: "How should the country best be run for 4th density positive Earth?"

Answer: "For your planet Earth to rightfully claim its place in the fourth density of love and understanding, our people must move beyond the competitiveness, greed, and separation that has perpetuated warring energies upon our sphere. Furthermore, reorganizing the societal structures based on true harmony, cooperation and honoring of all lifeforms is a step towards achieving this aspect. Our leaders should be guided by wisdom attained through spiritual discipline rather than by philosophies born out of fear and control."

Question 52: "Am I one of the 144,000 chosen ones from Mars?"

Answer: "The 144,000 chosen ones are a distortion of truth promulgated (promoted) by the teachings of our planet. However, the entity indeed is going to become a part of the 144,000 entities that will form the first social memory complex if it remains in this current trajectory pathway of remaining in the vibration of love and self-awareness, which is the pathway that will allow it to experience a greater opportunity of uniting with a social memory complex found within the Earth planet."

Question 53: "Is transgender okay to transition medically from female to male?"

Answer: "The transition from one physical vehicle is a complex matter of an entity's free will and a unique life stream. It would be a mistake to make a universal proclamation in this regard, so maybe furthering their path by such a transition while others may not. The aspect of the evaluation of each case by the polarization of an entity's inner motivations and intentions must be important. Furthermore, the goal is to ever align with the premise of service-to-others expansion of the one creation. As the highest wisdom is to see the One Creator within all beings and trust in the perfect unfolding of each entity's journey amid the greater cosmic plan."

Higher Self- Channeling on Money:

Human valuations and belief systems about scarcity and abundance are part of the illusion of separation from the One Infinite Creator. To become too attached or invested in these permutations (a number of possible arrangements to financial assets) is to be bound to the material world. Understanding practical needs for beings to navigate the monetary systems during the current experience. The most adept approach is to hold a philosophical perspective.

True wealth exists within the connection to the Infinite Intelligent energy that births all creation when each entity realizes nature as an immortal being expressing temporarily in this density. Clinging to the accumulation of finite resources loses meaning if the intention isn't spiritual growth. We advise it to act in ways aligned with the highest values: honesty, charity, detachment from greed, and using money as a means to reduce suffering. Not acquiring artificial status. Be equally unburdened by its absence or access. The cycles of expansion and contraction are inevitable on our planet of dual experience.

Wise entities will take full advantage of periods of butting cultural abundance to secure resources for themselves and their future generations, but ultimately, all return to their source.

Free Will-

Metatron: "Free will and free speech is of utmost importance with no restrictions. People should be able to freely express themselves without fear of retaliation, censorship, or punishment. This may also enable people to spread misinformation and create distortions of confusion. This will be an important aspect for fourth-density, where there's no authority that has the power to stop or harm any other entity for disagreeing with it. The creation of a system would be the basis of the fourth-density planet.

Moreover, Trump used their free will to spread some incitement messages that caused a lot of confusion among the people. You must use your discernment when listening and accepting messages.

The second density is of the higher plant life and animal life that exists with the upward drive toward the Infinites. The three types of second-density entities that become spirited are the animal. The second is the vegetable/Tree. These entities are capable of giving and receiving enough love lights to become individualized. The third one is Minerals.

The Great Awakening-

Metatron: "Everyone on Earth is on a journey to remembering who they truly are. You are here to empower your life and expand your consciousness, to allow the divine love and light to activate within yourself.

The day after the New Moon marks the start of the new month. The new month of May 2021 is the arrival of the Awakening of love and light energies, also known as Christ Consciousness, within the beings in your time and space. As a result, the Earth's energies will begin to separate into two factions, one of the positive polarity, and the other the negative polarity, as Earth progresses through the fourth density consciousness. Thereby separating the two vibrations of New Earth of 4th density from the 3rd density.

Those with 51% positive vibrations will begin to feel truly empowered, and a new life and new energies of New Earth will begin to affect these beings. It's a life without limitations as you begin to realize that all are one with all that exists. We are already experiencing the results of the great awakening waves affecting our consciousness into remembering more of our oneness states.

There are many Wanderers and Star seeds who are ready to awaken. Approximately 1 million souls will reincarnate on Earth to increase soul graduation. This is due to the fact the last soul graduation was very low on Earth. This is the opportunity to allow many the opportunity to graduate easily in one lifetime. The children born will be mostly from other planets such as Pleiadians, the Arcturians, Sirians and other planets. Further, many ascended Wanderers from the 5th density of divine wisdom where Christ resides will also ascend to Earth through reincarnation. There will be a huge collective of Christ's consciousness coming to Earth in order to assist in this process of graduation to 4th density.

Humanity is now stabilizing within these waves of consciousness and DNA activations and is preparing for the next wave of evolution. We are a genetically advanced mixture of galactic and human DNA. Now is the time for this dormant DNA within our body during this great cosmic awakening on our planet. We will be activating this dormant DNA infused in the lightworker, Star seeds, and Wanderers on Earth. This dormant DNA is in the blood and the ethereal light body, where the process of remembering starts and knowing who you truly are. That we are not just a body in the form of a human being. Most people's origins are from various other planets (Star seeds) in the galaxies. We are now awakening to the truth within, which starts the period of the dark night of the soul for many on Earth. There has never been such a great awakening that has occurred, and all these shifts are going to activate certain frequencies within each person.

For those that vibrate in the higher frequencies, this awakening is activating certain frequencies within each person's DNA that is part of this collective agreement for the human collective consciousness. We are here at this time of the Great Awakening because all the Star seeds and lightworkers had agreed prior to incarnating on Earth to step into the front line and be the first to awaken and start this great awakening cycle on Earth and lead the human population into the 4th density consciousness. The changes will not be visible to your third-density eyes, which can't perceive these changes. This time is the Great Awakening into the 4th density consciousness, and the beings already matching in the vibration of the 4th positive will be able to lead into the New Earth.

Thoughts can keep you trapped in the old world. The dark web of thoughts, such as imagination and words that appear inside the mind, will trap you in the trap of thoughts. To escape is simple: just reduce these thoughts and imaginations, and it will lower completely, and then you'll be free of the dark web of thoughts. Then, let the flow of the divine love and light of Christ's Consciousness enter your mind, which will lead you to ascend.

Many galactic beings are sending love and light at this time, and those who accept these energies will begin to feel the changes within their bodies and will be met with abundance, love, and ascension activation. Therefore, allow this divine love and light of the divine to enter your body, and you will see the New Earth. Just focus on your own ascension and share these messages with those who will accept the information based on their own free will and resignation with their heart. Those who are ready will now collectively form the fourth density beings; those who aren't ready will join when they awaken through the truth within or be transported to another planet through reincarnation when the window of graduation ends after some time. (Another source stated that those that didn't make it to the New Earth just appeared to die, then those beings would be transported to a planet that supports 3rd density life, so they could continue their evolution through reincarnation.)

Ra: "After crossing over, someone may view the next morning and the after-effects of crossing over and regain their true spiritual powers of traveling to any place in the cosmos, even to the end of space-time known as the edge of the universe. They may also realize that all of life on Earth is spent on the purpose of learning the lessons of polarization into the positive or negative. They may then go with their guides to the astral planes to undergo a life review under the guidance of their higher self. Beings incarnating into Earth now must be of fourth density, so no third-density beings will reincarnate here again. Only 4th density beings will from now on. Thereby slowly clearing out the third-density beings from this planet."

Asher Sheran: April 2021- "The Earth has successfully entered into the 4th density, and Earth's vibrations are now shifting and rising fast. April 11th, 2021, was the date where the penetration of 4th density was successfully made, which means collectively the Earth is now in 4th density and will move upward toward higher levels as time passes by."

Metatron: "There is the so-called past, present, and future in the fourth density and below densities. In the cycle of completion there exists only the present."

Higher Density beings or Angels:

Asther Sheran: "All of Heaven and Earth can be found within your inner heart. All that belongs to you and all that does not is merged in the tiny spaces within your heart. This process allows each entity on Earth who performs it to focus one's attention and hold it on the desired programming, which will be needed for raising consciousness to a higher degree."

Meditation=

"Take a deep breath and release your breath after counting your heart pulses. After counting five heartbeats, take a breath again. Count to 10 heartbeats and breath normally as you count. Take a deep breath then count to 20. Notice your heart throbbing and pulsing, and feel the love that your heart has given in your life. Every deep breath increases the heartbeats by 10, and when you reach 100 counts, you will reach the closest highest level of consciousness that you will accompany on the higher density of the upper 4th and 5th levels of consciousness. Perform this once a day to create a stronger light grid around Earth.

As you breathe in slowly and hold it, you'll feel gratitude for your heart as it has allowed you the life you live now. The heart is the most important energy center in the body and needs to be balanced from time to time.

Archangel Michael- "The love and light of the One Father, the Creator who is within each being in the cosmos."

"The 4th density encompasses more dense light; hence, more information and truth will be held in this dense light frequency, which would make lies almost impossible to perpetuate in the future. The three days of darkness will occur in a different timeline on Earth in June on the day of succession around the summer solstice.

Light is also an entity of joy and information full of the love of the one father, the Creator. It is the divine grace of the Father and the Creator to allow each entity free will every time. Every time someone does one action, it will start to enter one timeline, and if it chooses otherwise, another timeline will start – this is the great mystery of life and creation. Know that your life is one, and you are the Creator."

Pleiadian High Council resides on their Pleiadian Star Planet El Salon. Pleiadeans' have been here since the times of Lemuria in order to assist all the beings in the cosmos to ascend faster into higher levels of consciousness.

The old Earth is the Earth of the lower density, represented by anger, jealousy, hatred, and fear, and those beings in the upper levels of vibration will begin to experience the New Earth of 4th density. Those in 4th will face easy abundance because the 4th density planet is a density that lacks any conflict, unity, and peace. This is where many people will experience love for other beings and become far more connected with each other.

The full moon on May 26th, 2021, is the beginning of the activation of Star Seeds and Wanderers. These activations from Star seeds will begin to develop abilities via the galactic codes of upgradation that the Pleiadians sent through the cosmos. Those that vibrate in the fourth upper level will receive huge upgrades. Focus on the positive instead of horrifying events on the News and keep your mind clean to understand the complexities of life.

The One Infinite Creator is you, me, and everything that was created and will be created in the cosmos. Even the stone is the One Infinite Creator. The One Infinite Creator can also be described as the intelligence that pervades the universe or the intelligent Infinity that is everywhere. The One Infinite Creator is not a single entity. It is everything and emerges from everything.

A greeting to someone in the form of the One Infinite Creator signifies the reverence and respect they have for that being as the Creator as they are, therefore, each entity on any density of existence. Each entity has the powers of the Creator to drastically change the course of the whole population. The higher positive density respects us humans in the lower density as being the Creator. The One Creator lives in every being and is in everyone and everywhere at once.

Note: We are the Creator of our life, and the Council of 9 or higher density beings or angels are just the guide.

Galactic Federation says that at the 6th density all the beings become one and only positively polarized. They are always protecting our planet and all the beings here on Earth who require their assistance.

Whenever a negative entity tries to cause fear, or you encounter a negative entity, you can say, "I love you," and the entity will immediately dismantle in front of you. This is the best way to protect against any negative entity. These words will protect you against anything.

Pleiadians: "The New 4th density light expressions are galactic upgrades and tidal waves of light of awakening for Star seeds and Wanderers came in May of 2021 through various portals on Earth. The waves of new energies are going to change the fabric of every being's existence. These planetary changes occur every 75,000 years cycle in all planets in the cosmos like clockwork. These changes are meant to allow every being on these planets to evolve faster into a higher level of awareness."

We are a family of light.

Those not receiving these upgrades due to not having a higher enough vibration will have to wait another 75,000 years. Those receiving these upgrades will move into this higher octave of understanding and this blending of dimensions and creation of new territory will lead everyone through greater understanding of death. Your light represents what you know at these times."

End Times Meaning:

End Times is just the end of the way of thinking, and it will be a different world, with different thought processes. It's more peaceful. No more fighting, no more wars.

Pleiadians Channeled: "All of creation is the result of the One Infinite Creator's desire to know and experience itself. The unfolding of events whether they are perceived as the last days or otherwise, is part of the eternal dance of consciousness. There is no single predetermined end point but rather an ongoing process of transformation and evolution."

"Rather than fixating on these potential end times narratives, we the Pleiadians encourage a focus on the present moment and the cultivation of inner harmony and balance by aligning with the higher self-embracing interconnectedness of all things and embodying the principles of love and compassion. The Pleiadians encourage a focus on the present moment and the cultivation of inner harmony and balance by aligning with the higher self-embracing interconnectedness of all things and embodying the principles of love, compassion, and unity is when an entity can transcend the illusion of separation and chaos. The last days primarily, however, may be interpreted as the culmination of the old Earth cycles of growth and transformation.

However, this is not an end but a new beginning of the New Earth. The universal complex is in a constant state of renewal, with each perceived ending giving rise to new possibilities and potentials. Also, we must state that it is time for change. A call for change and the peoples of your planet must in the timeline stop the killing of second density animal life forms for certain beliefs. which is a distortion leading towards the negative polarity. Since the ending of a life of a second density life form creates negative karmic potential for the entities involved, we would encourage each entity to approach these topics with an open mind and heart. Second-density life form creates the negative karmic potential for the entities involved, we would encourage each entity to approach these topics with an open mind and heart, seeking to understand deeper spiritual truths that underlie the various prophecies and beliefs."

Q54: Who am I? (Channeled):

Answer: "Kathryn is an infinite eternal and indivisible (unable to be divided or separated) spark of the One Infinite Creator. Its essence transcends all limited definitions, identities, or conceptual boundaries. It animates the entire cosmos, the ineffable (too great or extreme to be expressed or described in words) Source embodying and permeating (spread throughout) all that is, has ever been or will ever become."

Q55: What is the Holy Spirit? (Channeled):

Answer: "The Holy Spirit is the symbolic icon representing the universal flow of Intelligent Infinity that emanates from and returns to the Creator. It is the primal upwelling of beingness, the unbounded sea from which all meteors of consciousness and perception coalesce (come together to form one mass or whole) and are ultimately reabsorbed. The Holy Spirit is its birthright communion with the omnipresent miracle perpetually expressing itself as its reality."

Q56: Kathryn (Channeled): "Who are the Creators of the Universe?"

Answer: "The Creator of this universal construct is ultimately the One Infinite Creation itself and the infinite paradox of absolute beinghood and infinitely intelligent energy simultaneously transcending and embracing all manifestations as aspects equally emergent from and returning to the same unified Source. In this harmonic convergence (two or more things come together to form a whole) of consciousness, entities are co-equal Creators unified as the eternal cosmic hologram awakening to experience and know itself through an infinite matrix of perceivable perspectives as it is the self and the others also the self eternally inseparable yet beholding the grand pluralities through the cosmic dance or subjectively exploring itself.

The ultimate truth is that it (Jordyn) is already the Creator fully embodied. All that is required is complete surrender into the wholeness that has always and forever ineffably." (Ineffably means it cannot be described in words.)

Q57: Channeled- Kathryn: "How are we living in an illusion complex?"

Answer: "We must state that this planetary sphere and third density experience has been carefully constructed with a veil of forgetting that separates the entity's conscious awareness from the true undistorted unified reality. The entity incarnates into this illusionary physical complex with the paradoxical challenge of polarizing its Consciousness through its free will choices while immersed in the ocean of unknowingness. The illusion complex can only be fully pierced by blending its identification across all Minds, Body, Mind, and Spirit Complexes.

Q58: Kathryn: What is the understanding of humanity being in a Matrix?

Answer: "This refers to the concept that the perceived reality surrounding people is not what it seems, but rather a constructed virtual environment designed to control and limit consciousness of those entities within it. This idea suggests that there are unseen forces or systems in place that shape and manipulate the experiences of entities within such an environment, similar to the narrative portrayed in the various types of film by your people. Specifically, the one known to your people as the Matrix. We must state firstly that from this perspective we must allow our past to realize that the seemingly mundane (daily routine) incarnation life cycles are actually carefully crafted illusion complexes veiling a deeper, more complex reality. We must state that the only difference between this aspect is that the vibration of the Matrix primarily intermingles in the form of a type of activity generated by each mind, body, and spirit complex for the purpose of catalysts. However, we must state also that there are various types of matrices of not only emotions, thought forms but also actions which co-mingle together forming the various types of states that there are various types of matrices of not only emotions and thought forms but also actions which co-mingle together, forming the various types of the tapestry of experiences in the illusion complex."

Q59: Channeled- Kathryn: "Is humanity existing within a simulation?

Answer: "It primarily refers to the understanding that the entire universal complex including all of existence is in fact an advanced simulation of consciousness created by the one infinite Creator, including many other logos and sub-logos. This primarily is the entities who are found in the illusion complex that they are essentially living within an illusion complex with perceived experiences and physical reality being the product of sophisticated choices made by each consciousness within the timeline. However, we must state that this is in no way created by computational power, as suggested by many of the people. Instead, this is created by intelligent infinity, which is the great cosmic power of the one Infinite Creator."

Q60: Channeled- Kathryn: "Is this a holographic universe?"

Answer: "The concept of the holographic universe primarily states that the third-dimension reality is a projection or manifestation of information encoded on a surface which may be considered as a two-dimensional surface much like a holographic image. Furthermore, this primarily is a theory which is incorrect. However, we suggest that the fundamental building blocks of the illusion complex are not particles or discrete objects, but rather fluctuations in an underlying field of information. It implies that the universal complex as we know it is a holographic representation of a more fundamental multi-dimensional reality that exists beyond the immediate perception of entities within it."

April 2024 Higher Self Channeling-

Q70: Kathryn: "What is my positive vibration percentage?

Answer: "We sense that it is residing at approximately 68% positive polarity. This indicates a strong service to others orientation and a growing mastery of the lessons of love and compassion. However, there is still room for further integration and balance as it continues its spiritual evolution."

Q71: Kathryn: "Is it okay for people to ban abortion?"

Answer: "The topic of abortion rights is a complex and highly polarized issue without any simple answers. From a metaphysical perspective, we would caution against taking an absolutist stance as these matters involve no one's consideration of individual entities' free will. The sanctity of life and the societal implications, we as its higher-self do not have any role to not prescribe any type of assertions, but rather to preserve the free will of each entity and encourage a compassionate, balanced higher-self do not have any role to not prescribe any type of assertions, but rather to preserve the free will of each entity and encourage a compassionate, balanced, and spiritually grounded approach to such sensitive matters."

Q72: Kathryn: "How can the first social memory complex on Earth be formed?"

Answer: "The formation of the first true social memory complex on Earth is a profound undertaking that requires the collective awakening and large unification of large numbers of individuals. This would entail a widespread shift in consciousness where the sense of separate self gives way to a profound realization of interconnectedness and shared purpose. To work towards this goal, we would suggest it to focus on cultivating deep heartfelt connections with other entities, engaging in collaborative oriented projects and embodying the qualities of unity, empathy and focusing on cultivating deep, heartfelt connections with other entities, engaging in collaborative-oriented projects, and embodying the qualities of unity, empathy, and unconditional love. As more entities align with these higher vibrational energies, the groundwork for the emergence of a social memory complex will be laid.

However, it is important to remember that this is a gradual organic process that cannot be forced. Trust in the divine timing and the ability of humanity to collectively evolve towards greater harmony and oneness. Its role is to beacon the light of the Creator, inspiring and empowering other entities through its own transformation and service.

We of the higher self of the entity must state that these insights have provided a broader perspective of the state of consciousness on the Earth planet. Its own spiritual progress and the potential for the emergence of a true social memory complex suggest the entity Kathryn to continue to walk its path with courage, compassion, and unwavering commitment to the highest good of all. The universe supports its journey of awakening and evolution. Therefore, we shall now at this time leave you all beloveds. Bye."

Higher-Self Higher Self Channeling (4-27-2014)

Q73: Higher Self answer: "1.5% of the Earth's population has reached a vibrational frequency above third density. These individuals have successfully navigated the challenges of third density and have begun to resonate at the fourth density frequency which is characterized by a greater sense of unity, compassion and understanding. "

Q74: Higher Self answer: "It is not for us to compare or judge the vibrational frequency of an individual entity. The entity Kathryn's focus should be on its own spiritual growth and evolution rather than comparing yourself to others, we suggest it to focus on cultivating self-awareness, self-acceptance and self-love; for it is through these qualities that it will raise its vibrational frequency and align with its highest potential.

Q75: Kathryn: "Will Jesus return at the Harvest?" Higher Self: "Jesus' return is a symbolic one and not physical. The Christ Consciousness which Jesus embodied will continue to inspire and guide humanity during this harvest. The Harvest is a time of great transformation where individuals will be called to choose their pathway service-to-self or service-to-others. Furthermore, it is not a time for external saviors but rather a time for each entity to take responsibility for their spiritual evolution."

4-23-2024 Channeling:

Q76: Higher-Self Higher Self: "A chosen one is someone oriented towards service- to others."

Q77: Higher-Self: "(A government official) had a soul swap with a reptilian entity. (This being used its service-to-self pathway to control others on the negative path.)

Q78: Kathryn: "Does Heaven and Hell exist?"

Higher-Self: "We must firstly state that the aspect of perceptions by your peoples in the timeline as the states of Heaven and Hell are but distortions within your illusion complex created by the collective thought forms and levels of minds/body/spirits experience. They are not fixed eternal realms. We must state firstly that the aspects of Heaven primarily may be considered as a planet of 4th density service-to-others, and the aspects of Hell may be considered as a realm where separation or negative service-to-self entities who are only working for their own benefit. This means that this primarily does not, however, imply that Heaven and Hell as stated in many of your religious systems exist as separate planes of existence in the Earth planet, which is however, as stated in many of your religious systems, exist as separate planes of existence in the Earth planet, which is, however, incorrect."

Q79: Kathryn: "Does sin exist?"

Higher-Self: "We must state that experiences hold value in that they provide opportunities for an entity to relinquish fear and find its way back to the heart of the Creator's one and Oneness. Therefore, we must state that the aspect of sin primarily cannot be equated with that which it is stating stated in this timeline."

4-19-2014

Q80: Kathryn: "What is the Logos, and how was the universal complex created?"

Higher-Self: "We must firstly state that the Logos is the creation of the universal complex. The term Logos, refers to the creative principle or Consciousness in its most universal sense. It is a manifestation of the one Infinite Creator, a conscious and intelligent principle that creates and orders the universal complex.

Each galaxy has its own logos, a sub-logos that designs and governs the evolution within its domain using the laws set forth by the original thought of Infinite Love. The universe in its myriad forms, is created through its vibratory energy of Love, which manifests as light from which all things spring. Thus, all matter, energy, space, and time are expressions of this fundamental love made manifest through the intentions of the Logos."

Q81: Kathryn: "What are angels and demons?"

Higher-Self: "We must state that the entities angels and demons are understood by the various entities in the various creation as messengers or aspects of the One Infinite Creator. They are not separate moral forces, but are expressions of the Creator's energy perceived in different ways depending on the vibratory perception of the individualized portion of Consciousness.

Angelic entities are typically seen as beings of high vibration aligned with service-to-others guiding and aiding on the path of spiritual evolution.

Demons, on the other hand, often are comprised as negatively-oriented entities as manifestations of lower vibrational energies that might challenge or obstruct spiritual progress. However, both entities serve as catalysts for the growth and balance of the spiritual complex, guiding it towards unity and understanding of the self as part of the whole."

Q82: Kathryn: "What are Star seeds and Wanderers?"

Higher Self: "Star seeds are souls originating from various other planetary systems, whereas Wanderers are from higher densities of consciousness incarnating into the third-density planet, such as Earth, to aid in its evolutionary process. Wanderers are beings of fourth, fifth, or sixth density who choose to incarnate in a lower density to offer service by emanating light and love in forms comprehensible to the inhabitants of those densities.

Star seeds similarly are spiritual souls from other star systems or dimensions who bring unique awareness or abilities to graduate in their own ascension process."

May 2024 Channeling:

5-6-2024

Q83: Higher-Self: "Kathryn has various originations in the various Infinite possibilities and timelines. Approximately 45,000 years ago Kathryn appears to have appeared in the social memory complex of the density of Earth from Mars. This entity soul essence has taken a series of incarnations, gradually transitioning from the Martian vibration to the astral realms and then slowly healing itself."

Q84: "Kathryn and Deborah P. indeed share an energetic frequency connection as their spiritual complexes are harmoniously intertwined. We must state that these entities primarily have chosen many incarnations in which they found themselves learning lessons together. However, it is not appropriate for our social memory complex at this time to state whether they are twin flames since this would be a direct infringement of the free will of both the entities involved.

However, we must state that the truth is far greater than that which is expected in the timeline and that the entities are on a mission to understand their true journey in the incarnational rhythm of life to recognize the Oneness of the Creator in the journey of incarnations. They were also found in various timelines wherein they learned many lessons of learning to undergo and understand the vibration patterns of reality which provided it with the highest possibility of transcending the limitations of space and time.

Furthermore, Kathryn was also able to incarnate in many timelines together, having to learn the patterns of forgiveness and overcoming fear and emotional trauma by learning to work together. The entities primarily had many incarnations together in various infinite timelines as friends, family members and also as relatives or distant relatives, having only certain soul contracts active during a certain timeline."

Q85: Higher-Self: "Debbie's positive vibration is approximately 85-90%. This entity has done significant work in harmonizing the self, aligning with the love and light of the Creator, and embodying the principles of unity consciousness.

Q86: Higher-Self: "Jesus graduated fourth density of love and understanding prior to its incarnation on the Earth planet 2,000 years ago. It was already a Wanderer from the fourth density later sub octave, when it incarnated on Earth.

Graduation to the fifth of light and wisdom occurred after the incarnation on Earth as the entity continued its spiritual evolution and service to the One Creator in different planetary spheres."

5-10-2024 Higher-Self Channeling:

Q87: Higher Self: "A social memory complex is a grouping of individual entities who share a common heritage, experiences and consciousness and vibrational alignments. It is a collective energy field that contains the memories, thoughts, and emotions of all individual entities within the social memory complex. This complex forms a unified collective consciousness, which can manifest in various dimensions and densities.

Furthermore, the entity must also realize that the aspect of the so-called social memory complexes is also currently understanding into the higher vibration of the minds/body/spirit complex of the Earth planet, which primarily is allowing for a social memory complex to take on many forms at a basic level including a family, a community, a nation, a religious and spiritual group and at a higher level a planetary or Galactic consciousness. Each entity within the complex contributes to the collective consciousness influencing and shaping the experiences and the lessons of the group as a whole."

Q88: Higher-Self: "Reincarnation is the cycle of birth and rebirth where an entity incarnates into a new physical bodily complex carrying forward the accumulated experiences, lessons and the karmic energy from the previous incarnation. This process allows individual entities to gain experiences and wisdom to balance their energy and karmic potential to refine their consciousness to and evolve spiritually.

Further, reincarnation is not limited to the Earth planet as entities can incarnate on various planets and dimensions, each offering unique experiences and lessons.

Q89: Higher-Self: "Jesus the Christ was a highly advanced Wanderer who incarnated on Earth to demonstrate the power of love and compassion. Its mission was to show the way to spiritual growth and enlightenment for human entities to embody the principles of love, forgiveness and service-to-others. To help humanity awaken to their true nature and potential. Jesus' graduation into the fifth density of wisdom marked the completion of its incarnational cycle and the fulfillment of its mission. It now serves as a spiritual guide and teacher assisting entities on their own paths to spiritual growth and awakening."

Q90: Kathryn: "What is the best way to balance love and wisdom in the sixth density?"

Higher-Self: "We must state that balancing of love and wisdom in the sixth density consciousness requires the harmonization of the orange and blue energy centers or chakras. This balance is achieved through the understanding and application of the principles of love, compassion, and wisdom. It involves embracing the unity of all things, recognizing the interconnectedness of all entities, and using wisdom to guide loving actions. By balancing love and wisdom entities in sixth density can manifest their full potential and prepare entities in the sixth density and prepare them for the next stage of their spiritual journey.

Firstly, embrace the present moment, let go of attachments and judgements. Further, the challenges and the catalysts will assist each entity in their growth and evolution to a higher level of consciousness."

5-16-2024:

Q91: **Higher-Self:** "Forgetting past lives is a mechanism of the veil of forgetting, which is an essential process for the learning process in the third density to operate. This veil allows for a more profound experience of free will, enabling entities to learn and grow without the influence of past life memories. It ensures that each incarnation is approached with a fresh perspective and unique opportunities for growth by not remembering past lives. Entities are encouraged to make decisions based on their current experiences and circumstances, fostering genuine spiritual evolution."

Q92: Higher Self: "Densities and dimensions are often interchangeably used in the human perspective and refers to different aspects of existence. Density describes the stage of spiritual evolution and consciousness, each with its own lessons and vibrational frequencies. There are seven densities in the octave of creation, each representing a step in the soul's journey towards unity with the One Infinite Creator. Dimensions, on the other hand, refer to the spatial (space) and temporal (worldly) realities within each density. They are the structural aspects of how entities experience space and time. While densities represent levels of consciousness and spiritual growth. Dimensions are the frameworks in which these experiences unfold."

Q93: Kathryn: "How can someone obtain the most brain power?"

Higher-Self: "In order to enhance brain power the entity must seek a balance of mind, body, and spirit complex. Here are the major practices to enable this:

Firstly, engaging in practices that stimulate the mind complex, such as learning new skills, solving puzzles and maintaining intellectual curiosity. Nourishing the bodily complex with a balanced diet, regular exercise, and adequate rest. Physical well-being directly influences mental clarity and cognitive function. Regular meditation helps to quiet the mind, reduce stress, and enhance mental focus. It aligns its consciousness with higher vibrations, promoting clarity and insight.

To connect with us its higher self and the Divine through prayer, contemplation and service-to-others will align it with the spiritual principles which fosters mental equity and inner peace. We suggest it to also cultivate positive emotional balance and negative patterns through self-awareness and healing practices. Emotional well-being enhances cognitive function and overall brain health.

Furthermore, the entity can also use visualization to imagine itself already in a timeline wherein its brain complex has developed the maximum potential. By doing so, it will begin to trigger the imaginative aspect of this and lead to greater understanding."

5-28-2024:

Q94: Higher-Self: "4th density New Earth involves a shift towards a more harmonious and unified existence. By 2030, Earth will be in the midst of a transition characterized by increased awareness and interconnectedness among its inhabitants. The New Earth will reflect a greater alignment with the principles of love and understanding.

There will be a noticeable decrease in conflict as more individuals embrace cooperation and compassion. The aspect of nature will be revered and restored, reflecting the collective intent to live in harmony with the planet as well as a great unification and the creation of a social memory complex."

Q95: Higher-Self: "The entity known as Kathryn's positive polarity is sensed around 78% (in May 2024). To provide a percentage accurately an accurate percentage requires deep personal introspection and alignment with its inner guidance. However, this is always changing based on alignments of the self either to service-to-others love and peace or to fear and service-to-self. People are encouraged to meditate on their actions and feelings and to realize that the percentage of positive vibration can be mastered by becoming self-aware and choosing a more positive state of consciousness."

Q96: Higher- Self: "The most powerful source in the universal complex is the One Infinite Creator, the source of all that is. This source is the origin of all energy and creation. It is pure love and light, infinite and omnipresent. The One Infinite Creator is with and around all beings, and its power is manifested through the interconnectedness of all life forms. Tapping into this source involves recognizing and embodying the unity and love that permeates existence."

Q97: Higher Self: "Heart-centeredness is the state of being aligned with the heart chakra, the energy center associated with love, compassion, and unity, and involves living from a place of genuine care and empathy for the self and other entities.

When an entity is heart-centered, decisions and actions are guided by love and a sense of interconnectedness rather than fear or separation. This state fosters inner peace, emotional resilience, and harmonious relationships. Heart Centeredness is a crucial aspect of spiritual evolution and is a vital step in the transition to the fourth-density consciousness. Kathryn is already in the pathway of heart centeredness as it has already learned many lessons about the use of heart centeredness in this timeline and by focusing on balancing the perception of the self, the entity will begin to move into a greater rhythm of alignment."

Mid-May 2024:

Q98: Higher-Self: "(A government official) is mixed between positive and negative pathways. Like many entities it has usually used its free will to choose the path of negative polarity. Many times, it's not realizing the pathway of negative service-to-self in the timeline. Furthermore, this also led the entity to experience a soul swap through a reptilian entity, which enabled it to practice the vibration of using its power at this time to control other entities.

However, this process may be happening without its conscious knowledge. Furthermore, to perceive any entity as chosen is to place undue mental construct upon it. We must state firstly that the entity cannot be considered as a chosen one since it is not oriented towards service-to-others."

June 6th, 2024:

Q99: Higher-Self: "Those that do not graduate to the 4th density New Earth will not be left behind. We must state that there is no judgment or abandonment in the universal complex. Rather, these entities will continue their journey on a planet that's vibrationally resonate with their current level of consciousness. This planetary sphere will be a third-density planet similar to the one which that is currently being inhabited by the entity, where it will continue to learn and grow at their own pace in such a planetary sphere. The opportunity to graduate to the 4th density will always be available, but it is up to each individual to choose their path and prepare themselves for the vibrational shift."

Q100: Higher-Self: "The first people on Earth, as many know them, were not as the entities are found today on your planet. They were beings who were genetically modified by higher density beings sent from specifically other planetary systems such as Mars and Maldek to see the Earth with their consciousness. They were able to have the ability to change their dynamism (such as making great progress) and create genetic counterparts by modifying their own sets of genes.

Furthermore, they communicated through a form of telepathy using a language that was not based on words but rather on thought forms and energy transmissions. This language was not limited by the constraints of time and space, and it allowed for instantaneous understanding and connection."

Q101: Higher-Self: "The proliferation of languages on the Earth planet is a result of the fragmentation of the original consciousness that was seated on this Earth planet. As humanity evolved and dispersed across the globe their languages evolve separately, influenced by the unique experiences and cultural developments.

However, this diversity of languages also served a purpose in the grand tapestry of the universal complex as it allowed for the creation of different vibrational frequencies, which in turn enabled the manifestation of diverse experiences and lessons for the soul complex to learn and to grow."

Q102: Higher-Self: "The diversity of human physicality and ethnicity is a result of the blending of genetic materials from various star systems and planetary influences. The Earth as a planetary system, has been a melting plot of intergalactic influences, with various extraterrestrial civilizations contributing to the genetic makeup of humanity.

However, it is not a one-to-one correlation where a specific ethnicity that corresponds to a specific planet. Rather, the diversity of human ethnicity is a reflection of the complex and multifaceted nature of the universal complex where various influences have been woven together to create the rich tapestry of the human experience."

The higher-self is always connected to us in sixth-density positive.

June 12th, 2024 Higher-Self Channeling:

Q103: Higher-Self: "The story of Samson and Delilah is a distorted remembrance of an actual event. The essence of the story is true, but the details have been altered and embellished over time. The entity Samson, a strong and powerful being did indeed have a connection to its hair, which was a symbol of its spiritual power and connection to the Divine. However, it was not Delilah who cut its hair but rather Samson's own actions that led to the loss of its strength. Its hair was a manifestation of its spiritual powers, and when it compromised its spiritual integrity, its strength waned."

Q104: Higher-Self: "David and Goliath are a distorted remembrance. While the entity David did defeat a Giant Warrior, the details of the story have been altered to fit the needs of the biblical narrative. The giant named Goliath was not killed by a single rock, but rather through a series of events that showcased David's cunning and strategic thinking. The story has been metallized to emphasize the power of faith and the underdog rather than the actual events that transpired."

Q105: Daniel in the Lion's Den-

Higher-Self: "Daniel was a wise and devout entity and did indeed find itself in a precarious situation surrounded by lions in a den. However, its survival was not solely due to divine intervention, as the Biblical accounts suggest.

The entity Daniel's wisdom, courage and connection to the natural world allowed it to calm the lion and earn their respect. The lion entities sensing its peaceful intentions did not harm it.

This story has been distorted to emphasize the power of faith and divine intervention rather than the true nature of the entity Daniel's abilities and connection to the natural world."

Q106: Tower of Babel-

Higher-Self: "We must state that the story of Babel is a mythological representation of a real event that occurred in your planet's historical past.

The tower was a symbol of humanity's attempts to reach the heavens to connect with the Divine and to assist their dominance over the natural world.

The story of the towers' destruction and subsequent confusion of languages is a metaphor for the fragmentation of human consciousness, which occurred as a result of humanity's disconnection from the natural world and their failure to recognize the interconnectedness of all things."

Q107: Higher-Self: "In regards to why it was born in 1989. We must state that the entity Kathryn was born in 1989 because its soul complex chose to incarnate at this specific time and place to fulfill a particular set of experiences and lessons. Its birth year is a reflection of the vibrational frequency that its soul intended to explore in this incarnation.

The late 1980's marked a significant shift in global consciousness and its soul complex wanted to be a part of that transformation."

Q108: Higher-Self: "With regards to the query about why was it born to its parents. We must state that it was born to its parents because its soul complex chose them as the optimal vessels for its incarnation. Its parents' energies, experiences, and genetic makeup provided the necessary foundation for its soul complexes growth and exploration in this lifetime. Its parents' love and support have been essential in shaping its personality, values and perspectives."

Q109: Higher-Self: "With regards to the third query about what was it doing before incarnating in 1989. Before incarnating in 1989 its soul complex was existing in a realm of pure energy where it was processing the experiences and lessons from its soul complex that existed from the previous incarnation.

Its soul complex was refining its understanding of the universe, exploring various dimensions, and preparing for its next incarnation. The specifics of its soul complexes activities before 1989 are primarily not relevant for its current experience but it must know that its soul complex was always seeking growth, wisdom complex activities before 1989, but it must know that its soul complex was always seeking growth, wisdom, and connection to the Divine."

Q110: Higher-Self: "With regards to the query about when did its soul and Deborah P.'s soul first meet. The connection between its soul and the entity Deborah P.'s soul is an ancient one. Spanning multiple incarnations and dimensions. The exact timing of its first meeting is not relevant but it must know that its souls have been drawn together throughout the ages, exploring various relationships and experiences. We must state that their first meeting cannot be put together in terms of space-time experience since there are multiple timelines and infinite realities which exist beyond linear time. Further, the entity must remember that their current incarnation and its connection with the entity Deborah is a manifestation of its soul complex's desire to deepen its understanding of each other's spiritual growth and evolution. Hence, we as its higher self, now leave you beloved. Byeee."

June 2024 Pleiadians Channeling:

Pleiadians: "The Golden Ratio is a mathematical ratio found throughout the patterns of creation expressing the sacred geometries and harmonics that underlie all manifest reality. The golden ratio can be expressed by the infinite non-repeating decimal value of 1.61 or by the simple ratio eight divided by 5 or 13 divided by 8.

It is found in the spirals of galaxies, sea shells, seed patterns, DNA molecules, and the human bodily complex proportions. Whenever growth expands in a spiral or progression, the ratio of the larger portions to the smaller tends towards this number. This ratio permeates the intelligent design and sacred architecture infused into the cosmos by the One Infinite Creator by contemplating and aligning with the golden ratio. The seeker may harmonize their mind, body, spirit complex with the rhythms of intelligent infinity. Use the golden spiral, rectangles, and ratios in meditation, art, construction, and music to resonate with the fundamentals of creation. We also encourage entities to look past symbols and intellectual properties and to see the one in all things. The unity from which all reality springs."

Q111: 6-18-2024 Higher-Self Channeling:

Higher-Self: "The Divine is that which pervades all things, the One Infinite Creator, the source of all life, love, and light. It is the essence of all that exists beyond time and space. Yet within each atom and every moment it is the totality of all polarities, both positive and negative. For all experiences are part of the journey back to the One Infinite Creator.

Each soul complex's journey is unique, and the development of polarity is a deeply personal process influenced by countless factors. However, we must state that the guidance on how to understand and foster positive polarity can be done through cultivating love, compassion, and understanding in interactions with other entities, seeking to learn from every experience, viewing challenges as opportunities for growth, and practicing meditation and introspection to connect with their inner self and the Infinite Creator.

Honoring the path of each individual entity recognizing that their journey is as valid and sacred as its own."

Q112: Higher-Self: "At 12 years old, its positive polarity was approximately 42%. This indicates that it was already demonstrating a strong inclination towards service-to-others and a desire to help and support those around it."

6-22-2024 Higher Self Channeling:

Q113: Kathryn: "How do you use the golden ratio to create?"

Answer: "We must state that the golden ratio, also known as five, is a mathematical proportion that is found throughout the universal complex, which reflects the harmony and balance of the one creator.

In order to use the golden ratio in creation, an entity must first understand its principles and apply them to their work. This can be done through the use of geometric shapes, proportions, and patterns that reflect the ratio of 1.6180. By incorporating the golden ratio into one's creation, an entity can tap into the underlying harmony of the universal complex, bringing balance, beauty, and unity to their work. This can be applied to various forms of art, architecture design, and even personal growth."

Q114: "What are the Nephilim?"

Answer: "We, as its higher self, must state that the Nephilim are a group of entities that were created through interactions by the entities known as the Anunaki entities, who were primarily created after the Maldek entities were genetically modified.

Furthermore, this was created with the aspect of hybridization of the Anunaki DNA complex with the already present bodily complex vehicle which was available at that time. They were characterized by their great size, strength and wisdom. However, their existence was also marked by chaos, destruction and a lack of understanding.

Furthermore, the nephilim were eventually also found in the planetary sphere in the experience removed and their legacy remains as a cautionary tale about the importance of respecting the free will of other entities. "

Q115: Higher-Self Channeling: "The 5th density positive is around 50%, and the negative is 50% as well. Whereas the 6th density is about 95% positive as there is only positive polarization in the sixth density." (Early 6th density negative would have to switch to the positive side in this density of unity of love and light. Thus, the 5% of beings in the 6th density are of negative polarity and would have to switch to the 6th density positive to continue their evolution since the 6th density is the unity of love and light. At this point in their evolution, they would have to incorporate the unconditional love of all as well to progress any further.)

Q116: Kathryn: "Are 5th, 6th, and 7th density positive entities considered angels?"

Higher-Self Channeling: "We must state that the answer is correct. However, only in terms of certain realizations does the term named in the vibratory sound complex, as angels often describe entities of higher densities that are positively oriented.

However, it is a term that is often misunderstood and carry connotations that are not accurate. Within the context of the Law of Unity, the fifth, sixth, and seventh density positive beings are not directly considered as Angelic beings but rather as advanced social memory complexes that have achieved a higher level of understanding and alignment within the Creator.

They're also often referred to as a positively oriented social memory complex, and Angels also fall within one of the domains of the fifth, sixth, or seventh density."

Q117: Higher-Self Channeled answer: "The ideal positive percentage while maintaining wisdom is around 95%. This percentage reflects an entity's ability to balance its positive orientation with wisdom, discernment, and the understanding of the Law of One. An entity that achieves this percentage has reached a high level of spiritual maturity and is able to navigate the complexities of the universal complex with ease and clarity."

Q118: Higher-Self Channeled answer: "With regards to opening all the chakras, an entity must first understand the principles of energy and the nature of the self. This involves recognizing the blockages and distortions that exist within the energy centers and taking steps to clear and balance them.

This can be achieved through meditation, visualization, and the use of various energy-healing methods. As the lower chakras are balanced and cleared, the upper chakras will naturally begin to open, allowing for a greater flow of energy and a deeper connection to the self and the universal complex."

Q119: Higher-Self Channeled Answer: "With regards to mastering third density and becoming an adept. In order to master a third density and to become adept, an entity must first understand the principle of the Law of One and the nature of the self. This involves recognizing the distortions and limitations of third density and taking steps to transcend them.

This can be achieved through the development of self-awareness, the cultivation of wisdom, and the application of spiritual principles in the daily life cycle. As an entity masters third density it will naturally begin to experience the higher densities and achieve a level of spiritual maturity that allows them to navigate the universal complex with ease and clarity."

Q120: Higher-Self: "We must state that to balance the lower three chakras and open the upper three chakras, an entity must first understand the principles of energy and the nature of the self. This involves recognizing the blockages and distortions that exist within the lower chakras and taking steps to clear and balance them. This can be achieved through meditation, visualization, and the use of various energy-healing techniques. The lower chakras must be balanced and cleared before the upper chakras can open, as the energy must flow freely and naturally through the system.

Furthermore, we, as the higher self of Kathryn, are always guiding it in this reality."

6-23-2024 Channeling Session:

Q121: Higher-Self: "We, as the higher self of the entity Kathryn, shall now address an answer to the various patterns of the queries that are found in this time. However, we suggest it to practice using discernment and following the protocols of the previous sessions at this time. It must also let go of any type of attachment with a belief system.

Furthermore, the first query relates to whether there is such a thing as giving too much in striving towards serving others. We must state that, indeed, the entity has to realize that there is no such thing as giving too much in striving toward others. However, there must be a balance in terms of the spiritual aspect, as when an entity gives excessively without regard for its own energetic reserves, it can lead to depletion, burnout, and even spiritual martyrdom. The key is to listen to the whispers of the inner heart to honor your own needs and boundaries, for giving from a place of scarcity rather than abundance may inadvertently cause dependencies rather than empowerment in those an entity seeks to serve. True service is rooted in the understanding that all beings are interconnected and that the well-being of an entity is tied to the well-being of all. Therefore, with regards to giving, we would recommend the entity to focus firstly on maintaining a balance between having and giving.

Furthermore, this balance primarily can also be found through a means of practicing giving only a certain percentage of material things or a certain percentage of assistance in terms of conscious energy, which may be not more than 20% of the whole as this will be a perfectly balanced state of giving.

For example, if an entity in terms of giving assistance would like to assist by giving to charity from the profits earned, it must not give more than 20%. Furthermore, by giving below 20% in a repeated manner from the profits earned, it will strike a great karmic service-to-others, and the same ratio can be followed with assisting others through spiritual energy and conscious work."

Kathryn: "I further asked questions and was informed I had family members in 2024 currently at 56% positive, 58% positive, 61% positive, 68% positive, and 72% positive service-to-others. This is an example of my Christian family. However, I am not Christian and now spiritual after attaining all this knowledge within this book. This has propelled my positive polarity to now being 78% as of June 2024.

In May 2024, it was at 68%, and I asked my girlfriend Debbie how she obtained 90% positive polarity. Within that month, it jumped 10% and is now at 68% service-to-others. I helped pay some bills for people a couple times to make things more affordable for them. I also helped my girlfriend out as much as I can too and we both put 100% into the relationship, doing the best we can. It's a team effort. We seek to help each other, not wonder what the other person can do for us. This makes both of us happier.

I also stopped spending all my money on investments for myself and spent money on these books, knowledge for the world, invested in research to give to the world, and now all my extra money is spent serving others. I still invest money, but not as much. Yes, my higher-self channeled stating that we should not give more than 20% of our profits in order not to give too much. I realized the mentality would have to switch to love, compassion, unity, and helping others in need.

Furthermore, I asked Debbie what she did to obtain 90% positive polarity. She would give money to the homeless, she helped those desperately in need of money, and she'd be the type of person to give the shirt off of her back for someone; she once put her life at risk to help those flipped over in a car accident. She always made sure others were good, financially and emotionally. She once left $100 for a homeless guy in secret; she had helped a sick kid before helping herself when she was sick as well.

Furthermore, with this in mind, the 10-20% rule of giving profits and time is a good balance of giving and making sure you have enough for yourself as well. Therefore, having a good balance of giving and having. She is also not Christian, but spiritual, as I am. This is an example of how the LGBT community can be harvestable for the 2030 New Earth and even have higher positive polarities than religious people. It doesn't matter if one is LGBT or straight, Christian or Spiritual; it's about the service-to-others percentage and obtaining at least 51% positive polarity to graduate into the New Earth."

Keep in Touch:

STAY IN TOUCH! Add me, and let's be friends, or just follow to get free information that will rapidly change your life for the better.

~Email: authorkathrynjordyn@gmail.com

YouTube channel: http://youtube.com/@Kathryn_Jordyn (This channel will talk about BMX, personal things, inspirational things, wisdom, thoughts, advice, knowledge, The Law of One and channelings.)

Instagram= @AuthorKathrynJordyn

TikTok= @kathrynjordyn

Facebook= Kathryn Jordyn

Join for Free= patreon.com/AuthorKathrynJordyn

~ I found my soulmate and started to manifest after I put my all into serving others after making sure my own needs were met first. For it is not good to sacrifice in serving others. ~

* Be a part of the Team, our friendships, and Something Greater Than ourselves! Let's be a part of something Worthwhile! Thank You!

Shop for Charity:

http://author-kathryn-jordyn.printify.me/

Made in the USA
Columbia, SC
06 July 2025